THE
DIGITAL
AGILE
LEADER

HOW TO ATTRACT, DEVELOP, AND RETAIN TOP TALENT IN AN EVER-CHANGING DIGITAL WORLD

MANISHA DHAWAN

The Agility Matrix™ is a pending trademark of Manisha Dhawan.
The Digital Agile Leader™ methodology is a pending trademark of Manisha Dhawan.
The FAIR Recognition™ model is a pending trademark of Manisha Dhawan.
The Amplify Your EI™ approach is a pending trademark of Manisha Dhawan.
The Culture Reset™ methodology is a pending trademark of Manisha Dhawan.
WD-40® is a registered trademark of WD-40 Manufacturing Company.
Bubble Wrap® is a registered trademark of Sealed Air Corporation.
Marvel Comics® is a registered trademark of Marvel Characters.
The Game of Life® is a registered trademark of Hasbro, Inc.

ISBN-13: 978-1-957651-37-8
Library of Congress Control Number: 2023905626

Designed by theBookDesigners

INDIE BOOKS INTERNATIONAL®, INC.
2511 WOODLANDS WAY
OCEANSIDE, CA 92054
www.indiebooksintl.com

DEDICATION

I consider myself more of a thinker than a writer. Yet the words *write a book* were etched in my bucket list for over a decade. I would glance over the list every year, thinking I would get to it someday.

In 2022, I decided it was time.

From organizing streams of consciousness to recalling and reliving major events, writing has been profound and cathartic. Through writing, I uncovered deeper layers of myself and strengthened relationships with the people I love.

Initially I was focused on completing my book when something unexpected happened. I watched my life replay through a different lens and with a newfound appreciation. Forgiveness, acceptance, and gratitude surfaced as I typed each word. There were moments of feeling stuck, followed by an outpouring of ideas. I had no choice but to trust and embrace the process.

This book is dedicated to my dad (Gulshan), mom (Rajni), brother (Manoj), and sisters (Anjli and Pallavi). All of them have been pivotal in helping me be where I am, and who I am today.

CONTENTS

PREFACE

We are in the midst of a renaissance where disruption is happening on a global scale and old paradigms are crumbling down to make way for the new. The world is changing and so is consciousness. This is not the first time in history, and it will not be the last. To survive and thrive in a new era, we need to learn, unlearn, and relearn new mindsets and behaviors.

In parallel, many of us are coming to a reckoning with our values, hopes, and dreams for ourselves, our loved ones, and the world at large.

As change continues, advancements across artificial intelligence, extended reality (XR), automation, quantum computing, and other technology will expand and evolve. The way we learn, live, and lead will shift in the coming years.

The question is: how prepared are you?

While there are many unknowns and we cannot always prepare for the unexpected, we can become more adept at anticipating, navigating, and embracing change.

This book is the culmination of over two decades of consulting, coaching, and leading digital transformation and change management initiatives for clients across different industries.

My purpose in writing this book is twofold:

1. To share lessons, strategies, and tools so you may feel empowered in the face of change.

2. To inspire more conscious, courageous, and agile leadership.

Throughout this book, I refer to "employers" and "employees" (note "employee" encompasses all talent, including full-time, part-time, consultants, contractors, freelancers, etc.). However, this book is not about employees versus employers. We do not want to create an "us versus them" mindset. We need to come together to solve the world's challenges and pave our way into the future.

Thank you for joining me on this journey. I hope you find my work helpful. As you read this book, take what resonates and leave the rest. Keep an open mind and reflect on how this may apply to your situation. While much is uncertain and remains to be seen, digital agile leadership can usher us into a brighter future.

1

THE CHANGING WORLD OF WORK

CHAPTER 1

WHY DIGITAL AGILE LEADERSHIP MATTERS

To thrive in the new world of work, you need to become a digital agile leader.

Digital agile leaders are self-aware, forward-thinking, curious, and adaptable. They question the status quo and have empathy for themselves and others. They recognize each person is on a unique journey of awareness, resistance, and acceptance.

Digital agile leaders are good listeners, question-askers, and big-picture thinkers. They understand that adaptability is chronic, not once-and-done. They are curious about technology and the change it can bring.

HOW MUCH TIME AT WORK?

One-third of a lifetime. This is the amount of time the average person spends at work.[1] As medical advancements prolong our life span, that duration could increase. Given how much time we spend at work, it makes sense to want some of that time to feel meaningful and enjoyable.

Yet, according to a 2022 Gallup survey, 60 percent of people are emotionally detached at work and 19 percent are miserable.[2]

Leaders can examine what is happening beneath the surface and evaluate if there are ways to make work more engaging, or at least *less miserable*.

With the rapid acceleration of technology combined with the pressure to influence societal change, leaders like you are grappling with how to attract, develop, and retain talent. There are many unknowns and no one-size-fits-all playbook. While you may not be able to retain every employee, you can take steps to improve the experience and lean into change. At the same time, you do not want to burn out and sacrifice your well-being.

How do you want to be remembered as a leader? How will you lead others through change?

NAVIGATING A CHANGING WORLD

The answers are not easy and neither is change. Think about what is changing in your life. Perhaps you are relocating, reinventing your-self, or reevaluating where you spend your time and energy. As you embark on a new path, you might look for signs of encouragement and ask yourself: *Where am I headed? How will life be different? Who do I want to be?*

As you drift through periods of intense transition, it can feel disorienting and overwhelming. Patterns are disrupted, routines crumble away, and emotions run heavy. During transition, you might need to rest, process your thoughts, and grieve loss. This could mean grieving the loss of a loved one, friendship, job, a time in your life, or "the way it was."

The world is in a continuous state of transition. It is normal to feel disappointed and unsure of where you fit in a new world. Despite any disappointments, you can find a renewed sense of hope and forge new beginnings. Again, the solutions are neither quick nor easy. It requires courage and strength to begin anew.

RISE, FALL, THEN RISE AGAIN

Michelle was recently promoted to senior director in a technology company. As she was getting ready one morning, she looked past her reflection in the mirror and pushed away uncomfortable emotions that surfaced. Finding coveted quiet time to process her emotions was challenging when she had other priorities. Besides, if she did not leave soon, she would miss her flight.

The year was 2022 and like billions of other people, Michelle had been through a whirlwind of disruption from the COVID-19 pandemic. The pandemic was one of several events destined or designed to shake up the world. The shakeup could be felt in every corner of the earth. It exposed and exacerbated mental health issues, long-standing inequities, supply chain deficiencies, and misinformation.

Yet, the pandemic was not the first global shakeup, and it will not be the last. From wars to plagues, injustices, and political unrest, it seems as if the world is in a constant state of upheaval. Beyond the pandemic, social and economic turmoil left people feeling blindsided and disheartened, as if we were regressing backward instead of progressing forward.

Despite the fallout, not all was lost. Opportunities for reinvention and innovation emerged. People made courageous life pivots and used their voices to inspire deeply rooted change.

LEADING THROUGH CHANGE

For Michelle, this was one of the hardest and most confusing times to be a leader. Leadership was not a new concept for Michelle but leading through high levels of volatility was unsettling. She was not sure how to address questions, such as: *How can we tackle new supply chain issues and competitive threats? How can the team be more collaborative and connected? How do we balance an increasing workload with well-being? How will we retain our people? What will happen in the future?*

After eating her usual oatmeal for breakfast, she made her way through the usual airport. Only, this time, things did not seem so usual. Something was different; it was in the air. The energy had shifted, and she was mulling over exactly what it was.

Could it be that more change was around the corner in her personal life, and she felt terrified? Or because the current situation demands more courage and agility than ever before?

How do I feel? she thought. *Scared? Yes. Disconnected, perhaps? Or languishing, I think?* The harsh realities of the world had engulfed her spirit and dulled the spark in her eyes. She was keenly aware of the shifting energy, and it became harder to feel hopeful. She did not want to feel like a failure and disappoint anyone.

Maybe I'm not cut out for this.

Michelle was accustomed to change but lately change seemed relentless. Beyond the multilayered trauma from global events, she experienced a painful divorce that left her emotionally devastated, newly single, and financially drained.

Michelle boldly decided to move across the country and start a new chapter. Each day, she rediscovered her identity and rebuilt her life. Some moments she felt lost, followed by days of hope and excitement for the future. Today was not one of those days.

Michelle glanced at a list of her goals, including paying off debt, buying a house, and building a family. It all seemed out of reach. As she boarded her flight, she felt exhausted, but she still had to show up for her team. Michelle gazed out the windows as the crew prepped the planes. Passengers boarded one by one, and she wondered, what was their story? When they returned home, where would they go next? Where would she?

CREATE A NEW PLAN

Over the next two weeks, Michelle's plan to launch a new initiative at work went completely sideways. Funding was slashed, projects were postponed, and the landscape was rapidly changing.

Michelle feared more good employees would leave when they heard the news, and realistically, she could not retain everyone. It did not help that the management team was fractured, causing additional strain on the culture.

The situation called for a new caliber of leadership and a new plan.

MOVING FORWARD

When I first met Michelle through a mutual friend, she was still mourning the loss of her old life when things seemed simpler.

We met at a quaint coffee shop near the coast, and dense fog had already blanketed the ground. She was in a mental fog as well, uncertain whether she should quit her job.

"How do you feel?" I asked.

"I feel like I'm in a boat and it used to be fun. But now the boat is sinking. There are more pinholes every day and I cannot seal them fast enough." We paused in mutual understanding. So much had changed, and it was overwhelming to think about what could be next.

"I'm good at what I do. Or at least, I used to be," she continued. "Lately I feel like my hands are tied and I don't even know if I like my job anymore."

After further dialogue and introspection, she decided to stick through it a while longer. She acknowledged the need to be flexible as things quickly changed.

"Wherever I go, I will encounter challenges. I want to try to turn things around before I throw in the towel."

I asked her to consider the following:

· What do you need? Where can you get it?
· How have you navigated change in the past?
· Get a pulse from the employees. What do they care about?
· Reframe what is happening. Is it a catastrophe or a setback?
· Where do you go from here?

· What would a new plan look like?
· How can you lead the team through this new lens?
· How can you take care of yourself in the process?

Michelle allotted time to improve her well-being. She started by going for a five-minute walk before work and sleeping one hour earlier each day. Sleep is important to recover and rebuild strength. One sleepless night can impair performance as much as a blood alcohol level of 0.10 percent, beyond the legal limit to drive.[3]

Even with these small steps, Michelle noticed big differences and felt better equipped to deal with the challenges ahead. She met with her team to develop a new baseline plan.

"We will get through these challenging times together and come out the other side even stronger and poised for success. This is going to require extraordinary collaboration and execution. I will work alongside you as we lay the foundation for our future growth."

The road ahead was still bumpy. But on the other side awaited new beginnings and opportunities.

MOVE THROUGH THE FOG

Leaders like you can have rough days. You might even have rough weeks, months, and years, and getting through the day is an accomplishment.

When you are headed in one direction, things can suddenly shift and knock you off your feet. As Michelle experienced, plans can go sideways and require an agile response.

If your plan goes sideways, what do you do? How can you find a sense of security and stability in a time of chaos? Try to find stability within yourself first. Take a moment to rest, reflect, and reprioritize. Seek support from others and figure out what a new plan might look like.

As the weight of the world grows heavy, it becomes increasingly difficult to show up as a leader. Trying to make sense of it all can be exhausting. Whatever emotions you feel, know that you are not alone. Be kind and compassionate with yourself and others as you navigate new waters.

Leading through change is hard. It is also a choice, a responsibility, and often a necessity. If you lead with courage, collaboration, and compassion, you can find your way through the fog. Perhaps this is idealistic, but it is my hope.

The premise of this book is that a digital agile leader can improve retention in the new world of work and lead effectively through change. The next chapters examine how leaders attract, develop, and retain talent.

TAKEAWAYS AND REFLECTIONS

CHANGE IS ONGOING. As you enter new phases of life, you may find extended periods of transition wear on you. Take time to rest and recover and find support along the way.

LEADERSHIP IS HARD. It is also a responsibility. Your ability to navigate change and bring others along is key. How can you show up better for yourself and others?

ALLOW YOURSELF TO FEEL. Consider any emotions you might be avoiding and how you can replenish your energy. Give yourself the time, space, and grace to process everything you have been through. Do the same for others.

SELF-CARE IS MORE THAN A BUZZWORD. It is an important tool in your arsenal to last as a leader. In a digital age, we are "always on" and connected to our devices. How can you establish better boundaries, disconnect, and recharge?

By demonstrating a commitment to self-care, you can model healthy behavior for others. Keep in mind practicing self-care does not mean to become self-centered.

CHAPTER 2

HOW TO USE MY AGILITY MATRIX FOR CHANGE LEADERSHIP

Kevin had served in the military for nearly two decades before transitioning to a career in the biotech industry. When he was a navy pilot, he strived to be a source of inspiration for his team. Time had erased most of the details, but he would never forget that fateful night at sea.

As he surveyed his surroundings from the aircraft, he saw ships perish into the ocean's abyss. Never before had he witnessed such flawless execution combined with fatal miscalculation.

Where had they gone wrong?

Darkness fell like a heavy curtain descending on the sky. Kevin had to land the aircraft on a small moving flight deck with only a few hundred feet of runway space. This took immense preparation, skill, and fearlessness. The winds made it extremely difficult, not to mention the pitch-black sky and looming fog. If he dropped in too quickly, he would miss the deck and be seconds away from death.

With intense concentration, Kevin clung on to any remaining morsel of hope, advanced the throttle, and skillfully landed the aircraft. It was a close call, as the starboard wheel came apart from the impact of touchdown.

Little did Kevin know how drastically his life would change after he retired from the navy. His transition from military to civilian life was fraught with challenges, including learning how to translate his skills and navigate a new environment.

In some ways, Kevin felt it was easier to be at sea, which he was trained to do, than embark on such a massive life transition. This underscores how change can be terrifying for *anyone*, even the bravest of leaders.

"When I started this civilian job, I had to think about what to wear each morning. In the military, we wear the same uniform every day," Kevin shared. "Even simple changes were hard at first."

Why is change hard? For many reasons. You might not have the support you need to navigate change. Perhaps the change was unexpected or unwelcome. Even a simple change can feel—well, not so simple. It requires your time and energy to weigh new decisions.

We are wired to resist change. It takes effort to go against our natural tendencies and break out of the status quo. With change comes uncertainty, discomfort, and fear of the unknown. However, as you know, change still happens whether we are ready or not.

BE HONEST WITH YOURSELF

After our initial conversation, Kevin asked me to help him navigate his career, which in his words was "falling apart at the seams." He had inherited a new team and wanted to optimize their efforts and lead them through change.

When we met later to discuss the results of his 360 Assessment, Kevin was disheartened to see some of the responses:

Abrasive. Dismissive. Condescending.

Each word punched a hole in his gut.

This is how I'm wired. Can I change? Do I even want to? What's wrong with who I am?

Kevin ignored all the empty chairs, preferring to stand up and lean against the wall instead. He fidgeted with the keys in his left pocket as his eyes flickered, rapidly scanning the room.

At that moment, Kevin had a vivid flashback of his childhood and how he learned to be independent at an early age. He cherished his grandparents' stories and fondly remembered how they would say precisely what was on their minds. Kevin felt electrified by their memory and reassured by the thought of home. He took another sip of his cold black coffee.

"I'm not *that* bad. I think I know who wrote that. It was Mark. He tends to be difficult, and I don't think he likes me."

After further discussion, he realized there was some truth to it. "I guess I could be doing more to bring people in instead of pushing them away. But my job is to get work done. That's why I'm here. I get paid to get results. I don't always have time for niceties. In the military, you have to deliver a message with razor-sharp precision. Or bad things could happen."

Kevin recalled the time an explosive device malfunctioned in the field. His comrade Camila shouted, "*Get down!*" There was no mincing, sugarcoating, or gift wrapping of words. Every second mattered.

Kevin made a good point. Clear and direct communication can mean the difference between life and death in certain situations. Besides, being direct was part of who he was and what he valued.

I could empathize with that. When a former manager danced around feedback, I told her, "Give it to me straight." That was not an invitation to punch me in the gut with hurtful words, but to be more specific so I knew what to work on. Giving and receiving constructive feedback requires trust, empathy, and awareness of potential biases.

Kevin proceeded to share some recent emails with me. "I would like to talk through these." He cast his eyes downward. "Can you help me brainstorm ways to improve my delivery?"

We discussed how he could adjust his approach to get better results and how adapting to communication is a two-way street. Everyone on the team could benefit from understanding their communication preferences and how to work well with others.

BE WILLING TO TRY ANOTHER APPROACH

Kevin decided to establish a monthly cross-functional meeting where team members could ask questions and learn from each other. We also talked about setting the tone for the meeting, so people would feel safe sharing concerns and challenging each other.

"We need to have open conversations as a team, talk through issues, and tackle them together. But it's hard to be vulnerable."

Kevin also wanted to add more warmth to his communications. We talked through specific examples and the importance of building trust. Even simple phrases can go a long way, including *thank you, how can I support you, what are your thoughts, tell me more,* and *I appreciate your efforts.*

Words are powerful, but they need to be backed by actions and behaviors. It is also important to contextualize communication, as there are different ideas of what is acceptable based on the relationship and the culture. If we expect everyone to communicate a certain way, we are setting ourselves up for disappointment and overlooking people's strengths.

As a sidenote, I do not condone changing your personality at the expense of your identity. It is important to evaluate your environment in relation to your personal goals and values.

Also consider how people might be downplaying their communication or code-switching. Code-switching means adjusting your speech and behavior to optimize the comfort of others in exchange for fair treatment.[4]

We all code-switch to some degree, based on where we are and who we are with. Marginalized people may regularly code-switch to feel safer and "fit in" with the dominant group; however, over time code-switching can lead to stress and self-suppression. While there are benefits to adapting to different environments, adapting should not be about hiding who you are.

FLEX YOUR STYLE

If you are a no-nonsense, no-BS leader, there is nothing inherently wrong with that. Being direct is helpful, especially when you need to clearly state your position.

Consider the situation and the audience. In some situations, it is good to be concise and direct; in other situations, taking a few seconds to insert warmth or even delaying your response can be helpful.

Also consider the communication method. When would a quick phone call be better than sending an email? Would it make sense to have a face-to-face conversation instead?

If I anticipate brainstorming or a lot of back-and-forth, I schedule a call. This way I can collect my thoughts and prepare for a more productive conversation. We are all different, so experiment with different approaches.

It is challenging to stretch outside our comfort zones, so give yourself and others empathy and space to learn.

INVEST IN EMPATHY

"I admit I don't always have time for empathy. I'm busy," Kevin stated candidly. The company was growing fast, and work-life *imbalance* was becoming the norm.

"What does being empathetic mean to you?" I asked.

"It means to stop and think about what the other person might be thinking. And to ask, not assume. I tried to do that this morning. I saw my colleague Lily and she looked upset. I asked her how she was doing. She proceeded to tell me, but I had to run to another meeting. Empathy takes time."

"Interesting. Tell me more."

"Well, I actually joined the meeting a few minutes early. If I had spent two more minutes with Lily, I might have helped her in a way that mattered." Kevin paused. "But there's only so much time in the day."

"Where are you spending your time?" He shared his calendar with me.

Well, that was the first problem. His calendar was double-, even triple-booked, and his unread email count was several hundred. We evaluated and optimized his calendar so he could find some breathing room. We also talked about how email was being used or overused as a communication method, and the prevalence and structure of meetings.

"What meetings are essential for you to attend?"

"All of them."

"What meetings can you delegate to others to attend on your behalf?"

"None of them."

This was going to be harder than I thought.

Kevin realized he was not fully tapping into his team's strengths and that he could delegate work differently.

OPTIMIZE THE WORK

Delegating can be difficult because while it might take you a few minutes to complete a task, it can take longer to explain it to someone else. You might want your team to demonstrate a certain level of proficiency before you delegate work. Or you feel bad putting pressure on your team, so you do the work. In the long run, delegating can give you time back.

Who you delegate work to is an important consideration. So is *what* you delegate and *why*. Why do you want to delegate a specific task? Is it to help someone learn or get it off your plate? Is everyone getting an opportunity to develop new skills and play to their strengths? How much do you trust your team to do the work? Delegating requires trust, patience, and clearly defining the tasks and desired outcomes.

Leaders often develop a job description or RACI matrix (responsible, accountable, consulted, and informed) to clarify roles and responsibilities across the team. While these documents are a helpful point of reference, the work comes alive in how people interact, negotiate, and execute. You can create RACIs ad nauseum, but there needs to be some flexibility and compromise in how the work gets done.

NO TIME TO THINK

One of the most common challenges I hear from leaders is that they are resource constrained and very busy. As a result, they do not have time for strategic thinking, and no one to delegate to. It is hard to be an effective leader when you do not have time to lead.

Given heavy workloads and limited resources, it is no wonder you feel stretched thin at times. Communicate with your manager and align on key priorities. Can you pull in other people to mitigate constraints and drive the plan forward? What are the top three things you want to accomplish each day? When can you take breaks to recharge?

TIME FOR HEALING

Kevin took a closer look at his calendar and blocked out twenty minutes at the start of the day. "This will be my thinking and planning time. I need a few minutes to strategize. I also need to make meetings more efficient."

As a leader, it can be challenging to determine the appropriate amount of communication and meetings based on the sheer volume of information. It is not about eliminating meetings altogether but connecting people and information more intentionally.

Be mindful of the clock, have an agenda, and provide additional channels to communicate afterward if needed. Consider the following:

What is the purpose of the meeting? What is the desired outcome? Who needs to be included?

Which meetings are redundant? What could be done asynchronously? Can a meeting be replaced with a chat?

What decisions need to be made? What information is needed to make these decisions? What topics can be tabled for later?

Who is dominating the conversation? Who is trying to get a word in edgewise? How can you keep the discussion on track while allowing it to flow naturally?

Facilitating meetings is more of an art than a science. You may not always be able to prevent a meeting from going off the rails, but you can guide the discussion and try to get things back on track.

MORE THAN WORK

Kevin continued to optimize team effectiveness and maintain an environment where people could do their best work.

Apart from leading a team, Kevin had more on his mind. He dreamed about rebuilding a relationship with his estranged son. They had not talked in years, and he could no longer ignore the tug in his heart beckoning him to reach out and communicate.

Kevin's heart had hardened over time, and facing more loss and rejection was painful. But he yearned for more joy in his life and was willing to take a risk.

"I may not know what the future holds, but if I try, I cannot fail."

Beyond career fulfillment, Kevin craved emotional and social fulfillment. It was time for healing and opening his heart again.

MY AGILITY MATRIX

Leadership is not for the faint of heart, especially as the demands of leaders are changing. Where have you been keeping your heart closed? What are you holding on to from the past that is preventing you from taking a risk and moving forward?

Sometimes we can get stuck in fear and disappointment, and it takes immense courage to escape from our mental prisons. Rather than give in to your fears, consider how you can take one step forward and gradually create change. You might take a few steps back, and do not be too hard on yourself if you do. It takes patience, courage, and persistence to face your fears and open your heart.

AGILITY MATRIX

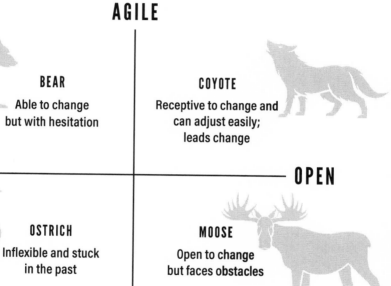

AGILE

BEAR
Able to change
but with hesitation

COYOTE
Receptive to change and
can adjust easily;
leads change

CLOSED ———————————————— **OPEN**

OSTRICH
Inflexible and stuck
in the past

MOOSE
Open to change
but faces obstacles

RIGID

I developed my Agility Matrix as a helpful tool to assess your openness to change and think about where you might be getting stuck. Each quadrant in the Agility Matrix contains distinctive characteristics represented by four animals: the Coyote, Moose, Bear, and Ostrich.

As I describe the matrix below, think about where you might fit when it comes to a specific change in your life.

TOP RIGHT QUADRANT: THE COYOTE

Let's start with the *top right quadrant*: Agile and Open. If you fall into this quadrant, you are receptive and can easily adjust to change. You are a change enthusiast and often lead the way.

Coyotes are considered one of the most adaptable animals in the world. Although we may view coyotes as pests, they play a vital role in restoring the ecosystem. As a Coyote, you are resourceful and can thrive in various environments. You are resilient and can alternate between being alone and in groups.

The Coyote might say things like:

I'm excited about this change.
How can we disrupt the status quo?
Let's test and see what we can learn.
What's another way?

As a Coyote, you are comfortable embracing and leading change, but you could leave others behind if you move too fast.

BOTTOM RIGHT QUADRANT: THE MOOSE

Moose are curious animals, but they can get stuck—literally. Sometimes their antlers get entangled, and they become trapped.

If you are in the *bottom right quadrant*, you are curious like the Moose and open to change, but you are getting stuck somewhere.

You may not have the resources or skills to navigate change. Your environment may be holding you back. You could run into additional obstacles and need support.

If you are a Moose, you might say things like:

I am open to change, but I feel stuck.
I need some help.
I keep running into obstacles.
I don't know where to start.

TOP LEFT QUADRANT: THE BEAR

Bears are highly intelligent animals, but they may be stubborn at times. Bears can adapt, but with some level of resentment, frustration, or judgment. If you are in the *top left quadrant*, you *can* change but do not want to. Perhaps your first instinct is to push back and become defensive or protective.

You go along with change, but you do not fully embrace it. There could be valid reasons and underlying concerns that make you pause. You might feel that certain risks have been minimized, so you hesitate to change.

If you identify with the Bear, you might say things like:

I can change, but I would rather not.
I am going along with this change, but I have reservations.
Before I change, I need more information (or motivation).
I've made the change, but I'm not fully aligned with it.

BOTTOM LEFT QUADRANT: THE OSTRICH

Ostriches feel comfortable with the status quo and change is hard for different reasons. Perhaps they spent years living a certain way and that becomes their worldview.

Ostriches tend to be tunnel visioned, focusing on one small area or perspective. They do not think they need to change, so they retreat, ignore, or avoid change. That does not mean something is wrong with them.

The Ostrich clings to the past even though the past is gone. They could struggle with change due to unprocessed trauma, stress, apathy, or fear. They may be living in denial with their head in the sand. Ostriches are at risk of becoming extinct if they do not evolve.

If you land in the *bottom left quadrant*, you are quite set in your ways.

The Ostrich may say things like:

This is how I've always done it.
I can't change.
I don't need to change.
Did something change?

START WITH YOURSELF

When it comes to change leadership, we need to start with ourselves. Examine your situation. What are your beliefs about a specific change? Where might you be getting stuck? What resources do you need? Where can you get them?

Maybe you find it difficult to let go of something. Try to identify what that is. It could be a job, relationship, past event, or mindset that no longer serves you.

My Agility Matrix can help you identify what might be getting in your way and what you need to accept or shift in your life. You may move across each quadrant at varying degrees during different cycles of change. You could relate to more than one quadrant at the same time. Do not judge yourself for where you are in the matrix; just bring awareness to it.

BRING OTHERS ALONG

You can use my Agility Matrix to discuss how your employees deal with change. Are they open to change? Why or why not? They may have valid reasons for resisting change. What do they specifically need to feel more supported? How can you drive more inclusive change, so people are not left behind?

It is important to note that people who *seem* closed off to change might not have access to resources. Do not assume someone's reluctance to participate in change is because they are resistant. Create a safe space where employees can share their concerns, so you can understand what might be getting in the way.

Clarify what the change means, discuss the impact, and develop a plan to move forward.

Whichever quadrant you are in, remember other people may be in different places. If you are a change agent, like the Coyote, it might not be best to approach an Ostrich and try to yank their head out of the sand. You might need to practice curiosity, patience, and acceptance. You could get better results if you build informal networks and focus on people who are more open to change. Conversely, if you identify with an Ostrich, you could try to learn more about a proposed change, even if you ultimately choose the status quo.

UNDERSTAND THE APPETITE FOR CHANGE

You might feel excited to implement change in an organization. However, you could face strong headwinds from teams who have established systems in place.

People may not be ready for change, even when shown the benefits. This does not mean your ideas will always fall flat; it may mean you need to establish credibility, garner support, and have a few wins under your belt before disrupting the status quo.

Focus on developing relationships and adjusting your approach. Be flexible, modify your vision of change, and collaborate with others. Who are your biggest supporters? Where can you show your value? How can you influence through relationships and establish credibility?

THE EIGHT KEY PRINCIPLES OF THE DIGITAL AGILE LEADER

Digital agile leaders recognize that the world is changing and there are opportunities to do things differently. Throughout this book, I will share stories and lessons learned in digital agile leadership.

A digital agile leader understands how to attract, develop, and retain top talent by following these eight principles:

- Shape The Culture

- Learn From Inside Stories

- Think Like A Scientist

- Connect To Purpose

- Co-create Career Paths

- Amplify Your EI (Emotional Intelligence)

- Believe In Belonging

- Play The Long Game

DEFINING AGILE

Digital agile leadership is not to be confused with the agile software methodology. While I have been on several waterfall, agile, and hybrid projects and believe there are pros and cons for each methodology, the focus here will be on developing agile *skill sets and mindsets.*

Agile means the ability to have a resourceful and adaptable character, or move with grace, like a dancer. Dancers are agile because they develop a strong core to endure twists and turns. Dancers can withstand rapid changes in movement and extend their range of motion while maintaining coordination and flexibility.

Note that agility is not about speed. There are risks with moving too quickly and reacting instead of responding to events. Agility is a more nuanced construct built upon cognitive and practical skills.[5]

DIGITAL AGILE LEADERSHIP IN ACTION

Digital agile leadership is about being adaptable and responsive in the face of change. We observed digital agile leadership during the pandemic when people made necessary adjustments.

People were agile as they reinvented their careers and made life transitions. Restaurants that lost indoor business expanded outdoor dining, take-out, delivery, and online ordering. Retail and other industries continue to respond to fluctuating inventory levels and changing consumer behaviors.

The healthcare industry bolstered telemedicine services, and manufacturing companies retooled their operations to create new products. When supply chain challenges wreaked havoc on production plans, responsive teams communicated with customers and found alternate solutions.

Digital agile leaders recognize that expected and unexpected events require a nimble response, with the flexibility to shift direction as needed. They know when to slow down and when to speed up. They are not just chasing the next shiny object and innovating for the sake of innovation. Yet they are open to exploring and reviewing new ideas in the context of their situation.

I wish I could say I became a digital agile leader overnight, but it is an intentional process and continues to be lifelong work. It has taken years of learning, unlearning, meeting *non-like-minded* people, and overcoming setbacks.

KEY COMPETENCIES OF A DIGITAL AGILE LEADER

A digital agile leader *CARES* as follows:

Curious. They are open to learning (and unlearning what they have learned as they acquire information and as things change). They are curious about the world and enjoy meeting people from different walks of life. They do not mind being wrong and admitting what they do not know. In fact, they welcome not being the smartest person in the room.

Adaptable. Digital agile leaders adapt to changing circumstances and new information. They recognize that while it is important to envision and plan for the future, it is also important to remain adaptable.

Resilient. To perservere through adversity and change, you need some level of resilience. Digital agile leaders may face obstacles and get demotivated at times, but they rest, reevaluate, and seek support to not only bounce back but also bounce forward. They can reconnect to hope even in the darkest of times.

Empathetic. Digital agile leaders lead with empathy and compassion. Leading with empathy means being aware of other people's needs and perspectives. But empathy is not always enough. You can extend empathy to compassion by taking action and helping others.

Strategic. Digital agile leaders do not change for the sake of change. They are analytical and strategic. They consider different scenarios and evaluate short- and long-term implications. They can see around corners and think systematically about how change can impact different areas.

CHANGE IS INEVITABLE

Change is everywhere. Looking closely at nature, we see transformation happening around us. Mountains undergo ongoing erosion and reshaping. Insects and other species metamorphosize and adapt to their environment.

Even language is a living entity that never stops evolving. Each year, an estimated eight hundred to one thousand new words are added to the English language, including new vocabulary in technology, pop culture, and healthcare.[6]

As the world awaits or incites the next wave of change, agility remains a key differentiator. Whichever way the pendulum swings and the power rests, keep in mind how we treat each other matters. When the next disruption arrives, how agile will you be?

TAKEAWAYS AND REFLECTIONS

THINGS ARE NOT THE WAY THEY WERE. The world continues to evolve, and we need to be flexible to navigate inevitable change.

GAUGE CHANGE RECEPTIVITY WITH MY AGILITY MATRIX. The Agility Matrix can be a helpful tool to build self-awareness and explore with others how they feel about a particular change. The matrix includes traits embodied in four animals: the Coyote, Moose, Bear, and Ostrich.

A DIGITAL AGILE LEADER CARES. They are Curious, Adaptable, Resilient, Empathetic, and Strategic.

AGILITY IS NOT ABOUT SPEED. Agility is about being responsive and flexible in the face of change.

EVALUATE HOW WORK IS GETTING DONE. Audit your schedule and tasks. What do you need to prioritize? Who is doing what? Why? How else can work be distributed?

MEET NON-LIKE-MINDED PEOPLE. You may naturally gravitate toward like-minded people, but growth happens in unfamiliar spaces. Make an effort to meet people you normally would not interact with and learn about their perspectives and challenges.

CHANGE IS A PROCESS. There is a natural process to cycle through change. As much as you may want to hurry up and skip the hard parts, some phases may be unavoidable and necessary for growth.

CHAPTER 3

MY DIGITAL AGILE LEADERSHIP STORY

As we discuss digital agile leadership, it may be helpful to give you some context about my journey.

I will never forget the day when Sarah, my former manager at a global consulting firm, was desperately choking for air. She frantically grabbed a notebook and scribbled something as her face grew pale. With her trembling hands, she turned the notebook around so we could see it.

"Stroke."

Sarah was having a stroke right then and there at the client site. She was in her forties, did not smoke, and was otherwise healthy. Within a few minutes, she was whisked away by an ambulance. Later that week, we received the news that she would take a leave of absence.

I reluctantly agreed when Chris, the engagement director, asked me to step into Sarah's role and lead the team. What exactly was I signing up for?

Chris was under a tremendous amount of pressure. Always in a hurry, his eyes darted about, looking for imminent danger. He was up for partner, and everything had to go right. That meant the pressure trickled down to us.

"What do you envision for this deliverable?" I asked.

"I don't know, just go figure it out," he replied briskly. I watched him disappear into the shadows, fleeting away like a gazelle.

His instructions were not exactly helpful. But they allowed me to do just that—figure it out. In consulting that is what you are expected to do. Figure it out, get it done, and do it well. Repeat.

The truth was Chris was too busy and removed from the details. He was fighting bigger battles and trying to win another engagement from a competing firm.

Stakes were high and time was scarce. Our inboxes would fill up faster than our coffee mugs and dinner drinks. The days and nights blended together. Weekly travel to the client site was par for the course. We did not have time to reflect; we just kept working. How we worked was normal and normalized. Take it or leave it, that was the job.

When we reached our milestones, we undoubtedly felt a sense of pride, followed by a strange emptiness and yearning for the next achievement. Staying busy kept us feeling productive and purposeful. We could conveniently abandon parts of our lives that were harder to face.

SIFT THROUGH THE NOISE

Throughout the project, there were endless fire drills. We had to sift through the noise and discern what was important, especially on multimillion-dollar projects where things can and do go wrong. Another high-priority ticket? Was it really urgent? What was the impact? Where should we focus our energy? How do we leverage the individual and collective strengths of the team?

Work was getting done but at the expense of well-being. I approved time-off requests for my team, knowing we had cross-trained for coverage as much as we could. Despite setbacks, we successfully launched the project on time and under budget. Building trust was paramount to success. Leading by example was critical; otherwise chaos would ensue, or worse—nothing would get done.

FROM THE BEGINNING

I have always been a naturally curious person and asked questions. It runs in the family. At the dinner table, we would discuss global events and encourage divergent thinking. My younger sister was studying to be a lawyer, and my brother was a high school speech and debate champion. As you can imagine, the conversations were quite lively.

I would question the status quo—not to be difficult—but because I was genuinely curious. My fifth-grade teacher would be visibly annoyed when I would ask a few whys in a row. At times, my questions were met with raised eyebrows and unamused tones of, "Well, this is just how it is." I never stopped asking questions. It became one of my greatest strengths.

BET ON YOURSELF

My parents were born in India and were refugees during the Great Partition. Millions of people fled unimaginable violence during the partition, uprooted their lives, and left everything behind. Fortunately, my parents and their families made it out alive. From already humble beginnings, they had to start again from nothing.

Education was the way to a better life. My father studied chemical engineering at IIT Delhi, and my mother studied English literature. After they got married, they emigrated to Canada, where I was born. My mother focused on taking care of our family, which gave her more fulfillment than any other job.

After a few years in Canada, we moved to the US. It was not long before my father realized his dream was to start his own business. Building a company was quite risky at the time since we were not in a good financial position, but he took a huge bet on himself and believed in his mission. He told me a few things I will never forget—have a good work ethic, get back up after you fall down, and never give up on yourself.

KEEP EXPLORING

Some of the most memorable moments I had as a child include watching my father build his company from the ground up in our garage. As a toddler, I followed him around the garage as if we were playing an endless game of imagination. Each time his phone rang, I would reach for my yellow plastic toy phone and pretend to answer the same way he did. He even set up a small desk for me in the corner that I cluttered with crayons and drawings of our adventures.

I was fascinated by what he was building and wanted to be a part of it. For all I knew at the time, he was building spaceships. As it turns out, he was building water treatment equipment. Even cooler.

During high school summers, my siblings and I worked in the family business. From administrative tasks to packing orders, no job was too big or small. I printed labels and carefully affixed them to file cabinets and shelves. I entered orders into the system, walked around the shop floor, and observed the manufacturing process.

After graduating college with a chemistry degree, I joined the family business again, this time in a bigger capacity. I was fortunate to be in a safe space. Safety did not mean comfort. It meant I was empowered to make bold decisions, experiment, and learn. This sparked a relentless drive in me to solve even more complex problems.

I asked a lot of questions (of course), observed, raised my hand for different assignments, and tried my best. Bright-eyed and eager, I wanted to make an impact early on. It was critical to understand and appreciate the company's history and respect why things were done a certain way.

"Dad, what if we tried this?" I flipped to a page in my notebook and pointed to a sketch.

"Sure, how do you plan to do that?" he asked, prompting me to think further.

We would discuss ideas, then I would go back to my desk, research, and formulate a plan. From the beginning, I felt purposeful. I was constantly learning, growing, and being exposed to new concepts.

My desire to continually learn led me down a path to get an MBA, followed by a career in consulting. I did not know if consulting was the right next step for me. My father was the first to encourage me.

"Of course, it would be great if you stayed, but I think this is an incredible opportunity for you. Go and try it. You can always come back."

Among many lessons, my father taught me to have the desire to explore, even if I find out later it is not what I want. After working with him in a supportive environment, I was about to get a harsh reality check. I was no longer in the family business and had a lot more to learn.

THE CONSULTING YEARS

As I approached the skyscraper, my eyes widened with excitement and disbelief. The building towered into the clouds, its mirrored windows reflecting the skyline.

I arrived at the conference room and started a week of onboarding and training at a Big Four consulting firm. A swath of other consultants zigzagged across the main floor and scurried to their seats. Leather-bound portfolios and ballpoint pens awaited us at each table.

Networking was an important part of training. I started by saying a few hellos to people next to me until I became acquainted with the cohort. At first, networking felt like an awkward and contrived activity.

I reframed networking to mean having a nice conversation, which took the pressure off. Networking can happen anywhere—from grocery stores to family gatherings and social events. Sometimes, I would meet someone and never see them again. Other times, people would reappear later in life, seemingly out of nowhere.

Networking is full of gifts and surprises. Paying it forward and helping others can come back tenfold in unexpected ways. Serendipity has a strange way of surfacing, and the more I networked, the more I realized how interconnected we all are.

A DAY IN THE LIFE OF CONSULTING

Networking is only one part of a consultant's role. If you ask a consultant what they do, you will likely hear, "It depends." The day-to-day is highly variable. Things are constantly changing, so you must be willing to be flexible and not get too attached to outcomes.

I still recall some interview questions:

- How do you create a shared vision when all parties are on different pages?

- When have you solved a problem using a completely new approach?

- Have you worked without any clear directions, and what happened?

ADAPT ALWAYS

From the start, my adaptability muscles were fired up and continued to grow. Adaptability was key. Adapting to changing requirements, flights, technologies, and environments. Adapting to working in airports, shared cubicles, and hotel lobbies.

Adapt or perish. It was a way of life.

As leaders respond to increasingly complex challenges—including supply chain issues, economic fluctuations, shifting consumer behaviors, and security threats—they need to be more adaptable than ever.

Studies have shown a positive relationship between adaptability and life satisfaction. While adapting to new environments can be difficult, self-adjustment and external support can help.[7]

Does adaptability come more naturally to some people, or can it be learned? I believe both to be true.

We are all wired differently. Some people prefer a slow and steady approach with clearly defined rules, while others thrive in uncertainty. People who are less adaptable might need more time to feel comfortable with change.

START ANYTIME

To strengthen your adaptability muscles, you can mix up your routine, explore new ideas, and surround yourself with other explorers. You can ask questions and experiment, give yourself permission to fail, and learn from mistakes.

Learning starts well before we enter the workplace, in our schools and homes. I was fortunate to be exposed to these skills at an early age, which shaped my outlook and gave me a launching pad into the ambiguous world of work. While it can be beneficial to build these skills earlier in life, not everyone may have this privilege. I hope we will collectively address the accessibility and skills gaps across different communities. A failure to do so will only further widen the gaps.

Schools can empower learners to become future digital agile leaders. Corporations can also be fertile grounds for upskilling and reskilling the workforce. We also need to have agency over our lives and invest in our growth where possible.

ANOTHER PIVOT

After two decades in the corporate arena, I was ready to serve in a different way. I obtained my coaching accreditation, followed my father's entrepreneurial footsteps, and started my own practice. My path was not linear nor easy, and I would need to pave it intentionally.

How are you paving the way intentionally in your life? How can you bring others along?

Below are a few key takeaways that could help you along your journey.

TAKEAWAYS AND REFLECTIONS

BET ON YOURSELF. Be willing to explore and take a chance on yourself. As you explore different paths, you can expand your ability to adapt and navigate new situations. This can feel scary but you do not have to do it alone.

TAKE INITIATIVE. You do not necessarily need specific experience to lead a project. What you need is a willingness to learn and get up to speed quickly. This means meeting with people, asking thoughtful questions, doing research, having a point of view, and keeping an open mind.

BE WILLING TO ADMIT WHAT YOU DO NOT KNOW AND BE WILLING TO BE WRONG. You do not have to have all the answers. When you feel stuck, ask yourself: *What else can I try? What do I need right now? Where can I get help?*

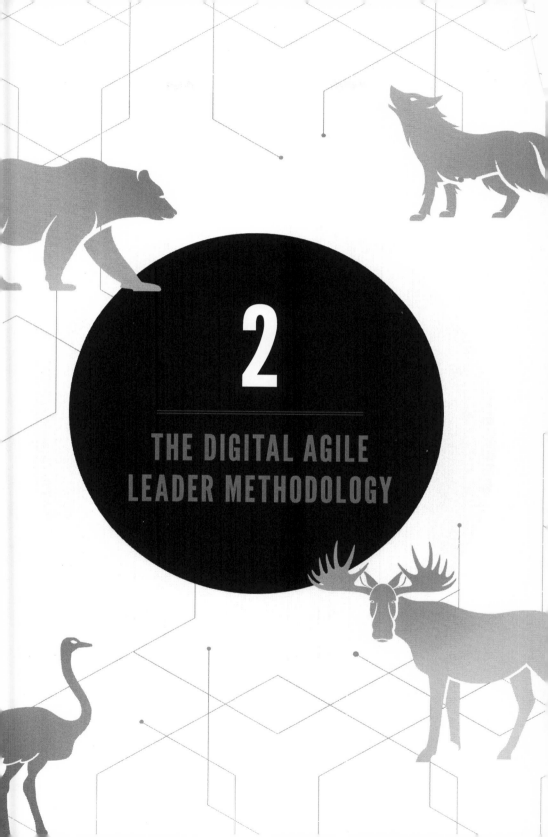

2

THE DIGITAL AGILE LEADER METHODOLOGY

CHAPTER 4

SHAPE THE CULTURE

Meena walked out the door with a heavy heart and a box full of belongings. Her manager looked in her direction, surprised by the turn of events. This was years before the "great resignation" (or "great awakening" as I like to call it). The year was 2015, and the company was about to witness a mass exodus, starting with Meena.

Meena had felt disengaged for a while. But disengagement did not happen overnight; it was over weeks and months, and the signs were there. She had expressed some of her concerns to no avail. Even though Meena still showed up and put in the effort as best as she could, her excitement had dwindled.

It was a bittersweet last day. On the one hand, Meena was going to miss the people—well, most of them. On the other hand, she had felt a surge of relief. She was ready for the next chapter.

Best Place To Work. Employer Of Choice. People First.

Meena stared at the wall on her way out, and something felt amiss. The words were in plain sight, but she never connected to them. They did not feel real or alive in the company.

Meena continually felt overlooked and undervalued. She started to doubt her abilities. Her manager took credit for her work and blocked access to opportunities. Meena wanted to grow in the company, but her manager did not make it easy.

It was not just her manager who got in the way, however; the issues were systemic. Meena did not have access to mentorship and was told to "stay in her lane." If she showed up with confidence, she was criticized for taking up too much space. If she was quiet, she was told to speak up more. It was a no-win situation and Meena was exhausted.

Publicly, the company was heralded for its culture. Those on the inside knew differently. At the time, it was a breeding ground for toxicity—constant reorganizations, turf wars, and even insider trading. Bad behaviors went unchecked, and HR felt powerless.

When the new CEO came in a year later, he cleaned house. He was known as the "turnaround CEO," which meant you better get your act together or start packing. He took drastic measures and axed 80 percent of the executive team.

Whispers echoed throughout the hallways as employees expressed how they felt about the changes. Their sentiments ranged across the board:

From optimistic: "This is exciting!"
To apathetic: "Whatever."
To skeptical: "Here we go again. I wonder what will be different this time?"

The company had seen a lot of attrition over the years and needed to rebuild from shaky ground. It took time to reshape the culture. How did it happen? With a desire to stop the bleeding, new leaders opened more channels for feedback, held each other accountable, and reset the culture.

DEFINING CULTURE

If you ask ten people to define culture, you may get ten different answers. In simplest terms, culture means how work gets done. This includes *how people treat each other* as work gets done. Culture embodies the energy of the people in the organization, the values, norms, and most importantly—the visible and not-so-visible behaviors.

Once the culture is established, it can be challenging but not impossible to change. In fact, it may be necessary to change the culture to survive and stay relevant.

FIVE TRUTHS ABOUT ORGANIZATIONAL CULTURE

Dynamic. Culture is a dynamic entity that can evolve.

Behaviorally Based. People's behaviors, and how those behaviors are rewarded or punished, influence the culture.

Experienced Differently. While everyone is responsible for creating the culture, it cascades from the top and can be experienced differently from the front line.

Divergent. Teams create their own subcultures and ways of working. Some teams do this better than others.

Requires Effort. Maintaining the desired culture requires ongoing, intentional, and visible effort.

WHAT ONCE WAS

I wish you could have been there the first time I met Amanda at a networking event. I did not want to leave the comforts of my home, but my intuition compelled me to go out. Perhaps you have experienced something similar. Your gut tells you to answer the call or go someplace, and suddenly, you are reminded how interesting life can be.

As chief people officer for a healthcare company, Amanda was dealing with a lot of uncertainty. Among other challenges, she shared how the culture was changing.

"Initially, we had built a unique forward-thinking culture. We were scrappy and nimble. We took some risks and moved quickly while also holding each other accountable.

"As the company grew, it became harder to scale and sustain our culture. I would like to think we are still innovative. Can you help us understand what is going on at a deeper level?"

Amanda brought me in to assess the culture, and the results were eye-opening. Employees rated the leadership team as out of touch, untrustworthy, and risk averse—the opposite of what the culture was supposed to be. Scores were especially low on communication, innovation, and making people feel valued. Amanda was disheartened to read some of the comments:

- "Leaders don't seem trustworthy." (Amanda took that one to heart)

- "We want to be innovative, but there is too much red tape to move quickly."

- "There is favoritism and lack of transparency."

We dug deeper to understand feedback for the entire leadership team, then developed a plan to address the issues and rebuild the culture.

CULTURE SHAPING IN ACTION

Culture can be a source of competitive advantage. In one study, 72 percent of senior management reported that their culture helps successful change initiatives to happen.[8] Amid change, organizations can seize the opportunity to rebuild culture rather than revert to the way things were.

Whether you create the culture or not, it still exists. This is why it is a good idea to intentionally create it by determining the vision, values, and mission, and then hire and train people around that.

The structure of teams can influence culture and how work gets done. A flatter structure can enhance cross-team collaboration. Too flat, however, and some employees may feel they are not getting enough mentorship and support.

THE CULTURE RESET APPROACH

To evaluate the culture at Amanda's organization, we took several key measures and followed my Culture Reset approach:

Review the company's mission and address gaps between the current and desired state. What is going on? Are leaders on the same page? If senior leadership is not aligned, that can create dysfunction. The realignment process takes work, including having difficult conversations and holding each other accountable. An outside facilitator can help.

Relate to employees. Ask them how they feel and what matters to them. How do employees experience the culture? What do they see?

Recognize the behaviors that help or harm the culture. When you see bad behavior, do you stand by or stand up? How are you rewarding stewards of the culture?

Revamp systems and processes that hinder the culture. The culture at Amanda's company was supposed to be nimble, yet work got done through multiple committees. We eliminated some committees and reorganized teams so they were more effective. What systems, structures, and processes impede your culture?

Reconnect with people. Employees want transparency. What findings will you share with them, and how will you turn their feedback into action?

Culture is an organization-wide effort and it stems from the top. Every person in the organization is responsible for creating moments that shape the culture. If senior leadership is fragmented, the culture can fall apart. Culture is a living entity, so it is important to regularly nurture and safeguard the culture by addressing anything that threatens its existence.

SAFEGUARD DOES NOT MEAN STIFLE

Safeguarding the culture does not mean creating echo chambers and eliminating conflict. Conflict is a natural part of working in teams. Most people do not like conflict, so they avoid it. However, avoiding conflict does not make it go away.

Not every disagreement between employees is a signal that the culture is toxic and needs policing. In fact, healthy disagreement could lead to more ideas and innovation. If you oversafeguard the culture, it can stifle creativity, add bureaucracy, and devalue employees.

How do you deal with conflict?

As a leader, you might want to stay out of conflict and hope the teams can resolve issues themselves. If they can do that, great. However, there may be times when you need to step in and reset expectations. It is important to get clarity and align on your core values.

AUTHENTIC SOMETIMES

Let's say authenticity is a core value. How do you define authenticity and to what degree is authenticity realistic in your workplace?

Vanessa, a senior manager at an energy company, prided herself in being an authentic leader but questioned if it was holding her back from advancing.

"We talk about authenticity as a linchpin of our culture, and I like to be real with my team. But then I get feedback to change my approach. So am I being *too* authentic for someone's preference? Is authenticity at your own risk here?"

Nina, on the other hand, did not want to be fully authentic and bring her whole self to work. "I am not close with my coworkers, and I prefer it that way. Sure, we get along, but that doesn't mean I am going to share all sides of myself. Only a few people get to see that."

53

THE DIGITAL AGILE LEADER

Authenticity is not possible without appropriate preconditions like a strong sense of trust in the organization and freedom from fear of retribution. Absent these, it is unrealistic to expect individuals to reveal otherwise hidden aspects of their character, viewpoints, or personal lives.[9]

If authenticity is a core value, consider what that means and how it could be unachievable and even exclude others. Not everyone wants to build deeper bonds with coworkers. Work is only one place to express ourselves; we have multiple sides of self and can decide when and with whom we share.

IDENTIFY TOXICITY

Even if you cannot see culture, it exists in the energy you bring and the environment you create. Take, for example, Briana, a senior VP at a medical device company. There was palatable tension in the air when Briana accepted an award without so much as a nod in her team's direction.

The CIO had hired Briana to lead the engineering team, and it was not long before she was butting heads with people. Briana was used to working in a hypercompetitive environment. She was enthusiastic and driven, which was an asset in some respects. However, she also demonstrated behaviors that undermined the team, including steamrolling her way through the organization, hoarding information, and excluding people from meetings.

At first, the CIO defended Briana. Deep down, he felt obligated to protect her since he brought her in and was invested in her success. Eventually, Briana parted ways with the company, but not before diminishing team morale and pushing a few good employees out the door.

It is not uncommon for leaders to defend their decisions. This does not mean leaders are not smart; it means they are human. As humans we have blind spots, and we make mistakes. Sometimes we do not want to admit our mistakes for fear of being seen as incompetent or weak. Yet, vulnerability can be a strength, provided the environment values genuine openness.

Being vulnerable is easier said than done. Perhaps you were vulnerable in the past and experienced backlash. There are risks to being vulnerable, and you might need to carefully select who you share with.[10] At the same time, if you are vulnerable, you can open channels for more authentic dialogue.

BE WILLING TO HAVE DIFFICULT CONVERSATIONS

You might hesitate to be vulnerable or admit you made a mistake, like hiring or promoting an underperforming employee. Consider what you learned from the experience and evaluate if the employee is coachable. Are they willing to reflect on their behaviors and make changes? Can you develop a plan to get things back on track quickly?

Here are some questions you can ask:

· Let's review some of the feedback you received. Take a moment to reflect and share your thoughts.

· How do you feel things are going?

55

- What do you think you need to work on? (*Discuss specific examples.*)

- Here are some suggestions. (*Emphasize the desired behaviors.*)

- How can I help?

APPROACH AS A COACH

When you ask questions and give people space to reflect, you approach them as a coach. What exactly does a coach do? They listen. A lot. They ask empowering questions and encourage critical thinking. When you approach someone as a coach, you can understand reasons for their behaviors and if they have a desire to change. Perhaps they lack self-awareness or need to adjust to a new culture. They may need to shed old habits or learn new skills.

While asking questions can be effective, in some situations being straightforward is the best approach. Employees do not always know what is expected of them. In industries where employees work with dangerous equipment, clarity trumps coaching. This does not mean the culture is toxic; it could mean the opposite—the company is diligent and cares about employee safety.

NOT EVERYTHING IS TOXIC

How do you define a toxic culture?

Be mindful of liberally labeling situations as "toxic." There is no perfect environment, and we need to learn how to deal with different people and situations. Whatever the case, if there is bullying, discrimination, or abuse, it requires prompt attention and zero tolerance.

People who are marginalized may experience microaggressions regularly. Microaggressions are automatic or unconscious insults or invalidations that send a message: *you do not belong here.* Although the prefix "micro" indicates small, over time these jabs could lead to feelings of self-doubt and exclusion.

But context matters and mistakes can happen. It is important for everyone to examine their biases and learn how to work with others. As a leader, you can set the tone for what is acceptable and speak up if you see egregious behavior.

Toxic cultures have undercurrents of negativity that can be draining over time. After working in a toxic environment long enough, you might start to forget what a healthy environment looks like. Like being in a bad relationship—you might justify that it could be worse, or it could get better. It may or may not.

Leaving a job is a personal choice and can be difficult for various reasons. Perhaps you have financial obligations, or your confidence has taken a hit. However, you could be loyal to a fault. Because self-worth is defined and derived by work, employees are at risk for experiencing Corporate Stockholm Syndrome, which can be defined as being loyal to an employer who mistreats them.[11]

If you are empowered to do something, speak up. If not, find someone who is. Exercise your ability to make a choice. Seek support, decide what is best for you, and acknowledge when it is time to move on.

RETHINK RECOGNITION

I first met Caleb when he joined a hospitality company as an IT director. We discussed the company's culture at length over lunch.

"I know we have an acronym with several principles." He paused and looked up at the sky. "No one remembers them all. I would say the culture is about recognition and collaboration. At least, that's what it is on paper."

Recognition was indeed a core value. Managers even had a personal award they would give to others. Since Caleb loved Marvel comics, his personal award was a superhero figurine. As he bestowed his award, he would praise the recipient for their hard work.

"I love superhero movies," he would say. "Thank you for being a superhero on our project."

Eighty percent of employees felt the personal awards were more about the giver than the recipient. And while some employees preferred public recognition, others would rather receive praise during smaller meetings.

While the efforts to instill a culture of recognition were admirable, there were opportunities to enhance the program further and provide FAIR recognition. FAIR recognition is:

For The Recipient. This means personalizing the award for the recipient (versus the giver) and understanding if they prefer private or public recognition.

Authentic. Recognition should be authentic and sincere. A few words of appreciation can go a long way.

Inclusive. While recognition is earned, evaluate who is being rewarded and who is being overlooked.

Real-Time. Show appreciation in the moment and not just at scheduled events. Encourage employees to recognize each other.

Consider all the possible ways to recognize employees, including nonmonetary and monetary reward options. Get creative. Would a points-based rewards system be feasible and effective? Could you give a day off to an employee if they worked long hours for two weeks straight? If so, how would other people view that? Should there be consistent standards across the board?

Recognition should not be a check-the-box activity. Who are you recognizing and why? Do you need to modify your recognition program to support different behaviors?

Note that recognition is not a substitute for respect. If you recognize your employees but fall short in integrity or take credit for their work, then recognition can feel manipulative.

GET REAL

The pressure to provide recognition, flexibility, purpose, and a sense of belonging can be a lot for an employer to sustain. While it is difficult to meet everyone's expectations, it remains important to be honest about what you *can* do. What are the biggest concerns your employees have? What matters most, and where do you want to focus your efforts? What would make the biggest impact on the culture?

DIGITAL AGILE LEADER LESSON
When you cannot be everything to everyone, be genuine.
Focus on what you can do now.

It is possible as a company grows, downsizes, or shifts direction, the culture no longer fits current-day challenges. Some cultures are resilient and can stand the test of time, while others need to be reinvented to remain relevant. What works in one organization may not work in another.

If you want to inspire a nimble, innovative culture, live it out loud. Infuse culture into daily conversations and actions. This could mean asking questions like:

- What problem are you trying to solve?
- How do you know it is a problem?
- How can you quickly test this idea and get insights?

Perks like onsite gyms and ping-pong tables can be fun, but they do not equate to culture.

"I never use the gym," said Linh. "It's nice we have one, but it doesn't mean anything to me."

"I'd rather have the time back on my calendar than feel obligated to go to another happy hour," said Jason. He had a preference for introversion, and the thought of going to another event sounded less appealing to him than getting a root canal.

Culture is less about perks and more about how people feel in their environment and how they can or cannot get work done. If employees are micromanaged or belittled, happy hours and free pizza will not assuage that.

MANAGE MICROMANAGING

"I don't want to micromanage my team. But I have to," said Kasey, a director at a creative agency. "It's the only way I feel confident that my team is delivering to expectations."

Micromanaging is an interesting topic. On the one hand, leaders need to let go of control and trust their employees. On the other hand, employees need to *earn trust* and show they can get work done with minimal oversight. Earning trust means being consistent and reliable.

Kasey had worked her way to sales director in a short time frame. She had a particular way of working with proven results. But not every client or project was the same, and there were alternate ways to achieve even bigger wins. After further reflection, she realized only one employee needed extra support because he was new to the role.

"How do you provide feedback?" I asked.

"I'm pretty busy, so I just tell him where he needs to make corrections. But I wish he would check his work."

"This would be good feedback to give him," I suggested.

We talked about how she could give more specific and timely feedback. Gallup found that when managers provide weekly (versus annual) feedback, team members are 2.7 times more likely to be engaged at work.[12]

However, feedback can be empty and patronizing when you do not understand the work. Feedback can also be laced with biases, so it is important to create trust and recognize when you exert control over someone unfairly.

If you are on the receiving end of feedback, be open and listen.

61

It is okay to ask questions and seek clarity but try to do so from a place of curiosity. Then decide what you want to do with the feedback.

It is normal to feel defensive, especially if the feedback is misplaced or you feel singled out. That is why trust is important. When there is trust, people know you have their best interests at heart, even if your delivery is not perfect.

Without trust, work can feel like a losing battle and tug-of-war exercise.

LET GO OF CONTROL

You have probably heard of the tug-of-war exercise. In a tug-of-war, people pull on both ends of a single rope. The side that ends up with the rope wins, while the other side might fall flat on their face.

The rope can symbolize power, money, resources, or anything that one side wants from the other. As the battle lingers, people can feel upset, hurt, or frustrated, pulling the rope harder to gain control.

Sound familiar?

If you can let go of your grip on the rope just slightly, you may notice that instead of pulling back, people will naturally fall toward you. Think about how this small gesture of releasing control can serve you in your relationships.

Some managers are afraid of releasing control. They may have fought hard to gain ownership and relinquishing control feels scary. They might believe extra supervision will avert problems. However, excessive oversight could prevent teams from figuring out how to solve problems themselves which can demoralize high performers.

On high-visibility projects, the desire for control can increase exponentially. You may be fearful that something could go awry, and instinctively exert more control. Or you may be stretched thin and resort to micromanaging to get a handle on things quickly.

Of course, if there are ongoing mistakes or you see a problem ahead, then it makes sense to intervene. Resist the urge to micromanage and try to determine the root cause. Could some employees benefit from more training? Are certain people in the wrong role? Do they feel safe to ask you questions? Is there mutual trust?

As you cultivate more trust, you can ease up and release your grip. Keep in mind trust is a two-way street. If you build trust, employees are more likely to be open about their challenges. Similarly, if employees show they are trustworthy, they can earn more privileges.

Empower your team while still being involved. When you are *too* hands-off you might assume everything is okay when it is not. Periodically check in, review the work, and update systems and processes as needed.

Letting go of control requires trusting the person and their process. In regulated industries, it is not that straightforward. In this case, explain the importance of following procedures. Give clear, forward-looking, specific, actionable feedback. Be mindful of when, where, and how you deliver feedback.

ELEVATE THE CULTURE

Cultures are variable, even across companies in the same industry. Some cultures might be heavily process driven, while others are more flexible.

It is important to align on a shared vision for the organization. Employees also need to learn about, shape, and adapt to the culture (or decide it is not for them).

Cultures do not have to be toxic to warrant improvement. In fact, high-performing cultures can still benefit from more collaboration and cohesion. Consider opportunities for enhanced trust and harmony across your organization.

What would an even more collaborative culture look like? How can people work together more effectively and efficiently? Shaping the culture continuously is a healthy practice. And it starts with how you show up as a leader.

TAKEAWAYS AND REFLECTIONS

CULTURE MATTERS. Culture exists, whether you design it intentionally or let it create itself. Culture includes the behaviors you model and the systems you use to get work done.

CULTURE DOES NOT LIVE ON PAPER. It lives with people and their experiences. Connect with employees to understand how they are experiencing the culture.

CULTURE NEEDS NURTURING. Regularly tend to your culture. Emphasize and reward behaviors that align with cultural values.

CULTURE IS EVERYONE'S RESPONSIBILITY. You can influence the culture by how you choose to show up. While culture stems from everyone, those in a position of power can protect it and empower others.

CHAPTER 5

LEARN FROM INSIDE STORIES

The last time I went into a bookstore, I noticed titles such as *How To Quit Your Job* adorned one side of a shelf. The other side contained books such as *How To Retain Your Employees*. The irony was not lost on me.

As a coach, consultant, and facilitator, I hear stories from both sides of the shelf—the employees who are disengaged and the employers who want to attract and retain good talent.

A digital agile leader learns from diverse stories. Stories are powerful—they remind us of our connection and how there are multiple ways to view and experience life.

THE EMPLOYER PERSPECTIVE

I have had conversations with thousands of people over the years and learned much from their stories. Employers consistently tell me that attracting and retaining good talent is one of their top challenges.

Some employers take a proactive approach to drive retention. Other employers adopt a detached perspective and think employee attrition is part of doing business. People can and will cycle out of jobs. However, frequent employee turnover cycles are exhausting and expensive. They impact the morale, culture, and bottom line.

Some employers are ramping up investments in AI and automation in anticipation of shifting labor models. Still, the road ahead remains murky and riddled with landmines. We have learned that things can change quickly.

Employers shared additional challenges including the following:

More than a people shortage, there is a skills shortage. We need people who are agile, resilient, and adaptable. We are trying to upskill our workforce and reach a wider talent pool.

The world of work is shifting and we are trying to keep up. We want to remain an employer of choice and retain good employees. But we cannot always compete with bigger companies.

Not everyone can offer remote work. Remote work is hard to afford to everyone and in every industry. As work evolves, we want to keep pace, but we have limitations.

We need to be strategic. This might mean slowing down hiring and adjusting to the changing environment.

Culture matters. Our teams have never been busier, and this is contributing to burnout. We need to evaluate the workload and how work gets done.

We need good leaders *and* good employees. Leadership skills are important, and employees need to be flexible. Not everything will be handed on a silver platter.

Reimagining work requires trust from both parties and a willingness to be flexible. Depending on the industry and company size, employers will have different limits on what they can offer.

Beyond compensation, employers can create a culture where people want to stay because they feel valued and supported.

Being a leader comes with heavy responsibilities and difficult decisions. Digital agile leaders recognize their span of influence and how their actions can impact employees, their families, and the communities at large. They understand that leadership has far-reaching implications.

THE EMPLOYEE PERSPECTIVE

On the flip side, I also hear inside stories from my executive and career coaching clients. They want to build more confidence, advance their leadership skills, or pivot to new opportunities.

One afternoon, I was having lunch with a group of people. We shared stories about our travels and families. Naturally, work became the topic of conversation.

"Do you like what you do?" I asked. A pause usually follows.

Kristina, however, answered without hesitation. "Yes. I love what I do. I wake up every day excited to go to work. I feel heard, respected, and valued. We challenge each other and we get along as a team. I have autonomy and a good relationship with my manager."

"What is one thing you would like to change?"

"Nothing I can think of. After many years, I've finally found a role in the organization that aligns with my skills and goals. Is that weird?"

"No, but it's rare," Josh, a quality assurance analyst, interjected with skepticism. "My job is a means to an end. I've been doing the same thing for years. I'm good at what I do, and it gives me stability.

It would be nice if I could find more inspiration at work, but I can find it elsewhere."

I nodded in understanding. "When was the last time you felt inspired?"

"When I was learning something new. I can do what I do now in my sleep."

"If you could be doing something else, what would you do?"

"I'd be a chef and open a restaurant. Even though I can't cook well, I would have freedom and the challenge of something new."

"I agree," Carolyn chimed in. She was a senior business analyst at a start-up company. "My manager barely has time for me, and when we meet, it's empty feedback and no tangible discussion about my future. I don't have any visibility into my career path. I'm ready for more. But I don't think that's going to happen here." She shrugged her shoulders in defeat and sunk into her chair.

READY FOR MORE

From engineers to executives and everyone in between, common themes and sentiments emerged, including:

- I am ready for more but cannot seem to find it here.
- I feel bad for leaving my team. But I need to start thinking about what is best for me.
- I want to grow and develop my skills and I am not doing that here.
- I feel overlooked and undervalued. My confidence is decreasing.

· I am just going through the motions and waiting for something better to come along.

· I feel stagnant. I am trying to stay positive, but I am getting depressed.

· I feel like I am going in circles and facing the same unresolved issues again and again at the company. My passion has waned.

If we learn anything from inside stories, it is that we need to have more meaningful conversations with each other. We can learn what motivates people and why they stay or leave.

A survey of US workers showed that low pay, lack of opportunities for advancement, and feeling disrespected at work were among the top three reasons to leave a job.[13] Is wanting more money enough reason to leave a job? Of course. We all have different financial goals. Yet money only goes so far. There are other reasons employees stay, including career growth, stability, flexibility, and a good relationship with their manager and colleagues.

"I stay because I have autonomy in my job," said Andrea, a healthcare provider. "I like the people I work with, and I have flexibility with my schedule. I am learning a lot and feel like I'm making a difference."

When compensation can only go so far, how else can you enhance the employee experience or even redesign it altogether? In addition to regularly taking the pulse of employees, design thinking is a helpful approach to understanding pain points and challenges.

DESIGN THINK THE EXPERIENCE

I first learned about design thinking while working on a project with IDEO, the global agency that popularized design thinking. There is no single definition for design thinking; it is an idea, a strategy, a method, and a way of seeing the world.[14]

Design thinking is a nonlinear, iterative process. The five key phases of design thinking are:

- Empathize

- Define The Problem

- Ideate

- Prototype

- Test

Across design thinking, there are cycles of convergence and divergence. For example, when ideating, you diverge outward and come up with as many ideas as possible. Then you converge and select one or a few ideas to prototype.

Beyond the design thinking methodology, the underpinning mindsets are key. These include:

- Practice empathy

- Have a beginner's mindset

- Reframe problems

- Embrace ambiguity

- Have a bias toward action

We would start our innovation projects with empathy by observing customers, asking questions, and immersing ourselves in their environment. Throughout the process, we would learn about their pain points and define the problem we were trying to solve. Then we would brainstorm, prototype, test, and iterate different ideas.

Without empathy, you might solve the wrong problem or problems that do not exist. For instance, you might offer your employees more paid time off when their real pain point is lack of career development.

As you gather insights, you can start to understand the problem at a deeper level. Then, you can define the problem as a "how might we" statement. Below are some examples.

How might we:

- Improve the onboarding experience for new employees?

- Create a more collaborative environment across the sales and engineering teams?

- Redesign communication in a hybrid work environment?

Framing the problem as a *"How might we"* statement encourages collaborative design and exploration of different ideas. It is also helpful to adopt a beginner's mindset.

A BEGINNER'S MINDSET

The concept in Zen Buddhism known as *shoshin* and a related quote by Shunryu Suzuki explains the importance of having a beginner's mindset: "In the beginner's mind, there are many possibilities; in the expert's mind, there are few."

When you approach something from a beginner's mindset, you look at a situation from a lens of curiosity. By contrast, an expert's mindset could hamper your ability to learn something new. With an expert's mindset, you approach the situation from an *I-already-know* lens. Try to put your expertise aside and adopt a *what-is-something-new-I-can-learn* lens.

It can be challenging to implement design thinking across an organization. People tend to get excited about design thinking initially, especially during the ideation phase, then fall short on follow-through and execution as business priorities shift. As a result, enthusiasm may decline. Successful deployment requires leadership buy-in and a willingness to experiment.

While design thinking favors a "human-centered" approach, we need to also consider broader design implications. This can mean adopting a "planet-centered" approach.

You may need to redesign the experience and not just create incremental change. Otherwise, you could be compounding issues and bolting ideas onto broken systems. However, sometimes change happens on smaller scales, and it can still be significant and have network effects.

Whether people or systems need to change is an age-old debate. People create and participate in systems. Yet systems can prevent people from making meaningful progress. For instance, you could tell your employees to be safe, but if there are hazards in the system, then the chances of a safety incident increase.

JOURNEY MAPS

To redesign a system or process, we need to be open to change and practice empathy. Journey mapping is a useful tool to cultivate empathy.

Let's look at a candidate recruitment process as an example. Below is a journey map from the candidate's perspective, from initial contact through onboarding.

At each step, the candidate has different high and low emotional points. The candidate is excited at first; then their excitement dissipates when they go through a lengthy interview process. While your interview process may be effective and align with your values, it is still worth revisiting.

CANDIDATE JOURNEY

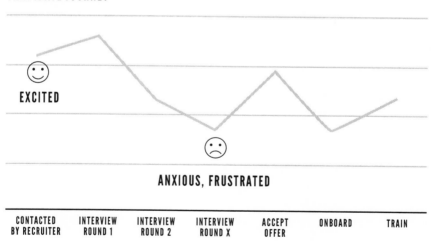

| CONTACTED BY RECRUITER | INTERVIEW ROUND 1 | INTERVIEW ROUND 2 | INTERVIEW ROUND X | ACCEPT OFFER | ONBOARD | TRAIN |

Invite people to share their perspectives and create their journey map with you. Through radical collaboration, you can design *with*, not just for people.

How might you redesign your employee experience?

TAKEAWAYS AND REFLECTIONS

CHANGE HAPPENS INTERNALLY AND EXTERNALLY. Sometimes you may need to spark change in your life rather than waiting for it to happen. Changing your internal perspective can trigger a change in your outside world (and vice versa).

LEARN FROM PEOPLE'S STORIES. Sharing stories takes courage and trust. Be willing to put your assumptions aside and objectively learn about other people's experiences.

DESIGN THINKING IS A POWERFUL PROBLEM-SOLVING AND PROBLEM-FINDING TOOL. Learn about design thinking mindsets and not just the methodology.

CONSIDER PEOPLE AND PLANET. As you innovate and solve problems, consider the broader implications of the design.

CHAPTER 6

THINK LIKE A SCIENTIST

I remember sitting on an uncomfortable metal stool in the chemistry lab for hours, carefully examining contents in the flask. Nothing seemed to be happening.

"The reaction could take more time," said the professor.

So, I waited.

I tried to focus on something else. We did not have mobile phones back then, so I was left to my own devices. I had to trust that the change was occurring, even at microscopic levels.

Sometimes I saw clear evidence that a chemical reaction was taking place, like when the solution immediately changed colors or transitioned from a liquid to a solid. Other times, it was hard to discern. Was something happening? Was change taking place? How could I be sure?

After several hours, something magical started to happen. The fluid turned into beautiful emerald-green crystals. Finally, I was getting somewhere.

EMBRACE THE CHALLENGE

I may have graduated with a chemistry degree, but I was not the best chemistry student by any stretch of the imagination. In fact, there were moments I questioned whether I should change my major. Like when I accidentally picked up radioactive samples with my fingers instead of using forceps. At least I was wearing gloves. Despite a few missteps, I persevered and started to enjoy the challenge of learning something difficult.

It is normal to shy away from anything where you think you might fail. But when things get tough, that is not always a sign to give up. It may mean to take a break, try another approach, or ask for help.

THE SCIENTIFIC APPROACH

As a chemistry student, I gained valuable insights that would unexpectedly carry over into the workplace.

I learned to think like a scientist.

Thinking like a scientist means to:

- Develop and test hypotheses
- Make detailed observations
- Experiment and learn
- Understand that change may be happening beneath the surface, beyond your line of sight

With each experiment, I followed the scientific approach:

1. **Identify the problem.** This is an important step. Often, people jump straight to solutions without first understanding the problem.

2. **Do research.** This includes having conversations, reviewing publications, and being mindful of biases that might come up during your research.

3. **Form a hypothesis.** The hypothesis does not have to be right. It is simply your best guess. It is important not to get attached to your hypothesis as things can change.

4. **Conduct an experiment.** Find ways to test your hypothesis. It is okay if you do not have a full-fledged lab or all the equipment you would like.

5. **Note down your observations.** Collect data and summarize your findings. From there, determine your next steps.

RETROSYNTHESIS

In organic chemistry class, we learned a powerful exercise called *retrosynthesis* (also known as retroactive synthesis or retrosynthetic analysis). We were shown a molecule and had to work our way back to determine its simplest form. Essentially, we had to "deconstruct" the molecule into its readily available starting materials. Deconstructing means taking something apart and understanding its basic composition.

Here are two examples of a retrosynthesis problem:

1. Using any chemistry you know, give an efficient synthesis of this molecule from start to finish.

2. How can the below transformation be accomplished?

You would need to figure out the steps, and there may be more than one correct answer or pathway. But you can choose a path—the most stable or reliable—whatever works for you.

Some questions to consider include:

- What do you already know?
- What starting materials do you need?
- What conditions could affect the reactions?
- What do you need to remove, add, or substitute to move to the next step?

· What could be a more reliable way to do the same transformation?

· Which path do you *want* to take?

THINKING LIKE A SCIENTIST IN ACTION

Thinking like a scientist can help you solve problems in new ways. Rather than implementing a major change at work, for instance, you can frame things as smaller experiments and gather feedback from your employees.

This could mean asking your team:

· What conditions are needed to create change?

· What can we start with?

· What is the desired end state?

· What smaller steps can get us there?

· What resources do we need?

· What questions should we be asking?

· What is another way?

Instead of starting from scratch, what do you already know? What tools and processes already exist? As the adage says, "You don't need to reinvent the wheel; you can just realign it."

Science is not perfect, and neither are we. Science is not always agile either. But modern science can be agile when you leverage existing models and collect data early and often to accelerate discovery.

MAKE SOMETHING NEW

You do not have to be a chemistry student to think like a scientist. Try this exercise. What can you create from the following?

- Burrito
- Salad
- Ice Cream

Probably not a lot unless you like ice cream in your burrito.

Now break them down into their ingredients and identify what you can make.

- Burrito: tortilla, cheese, rice, beans, onions, tomatoes
- Salad: goat cheese, balsamic dressing, arugula, apples, pecans
- Ice Cream: milk, cream, vanilla, sugar

With these separate ingredients, you can create a menu that includes goat cheese balsamic ice cream or apple pecan burritos. Chefs are like food scientists. They take culinary classics, break them down to their basic ingredients, and reconstruct them to make something new and unexpected.

METACOGNITION

When you think like a scientist, you can also enhance your meta-cognition skills. Metacognition means to think about what you are thinking about. This includes reflecting on questions such as:

- Why am I thinking this way?
- How do I know this is true?

· What if the opposite were true?

· What if I am wrong?

When thinking leads to overthinking and analysis paralysis, try to have a bias for action. This can be challenging for highly analytical or empathetic people who may need more time to process information. If that sounds like you, be kind to yourself, honor your strengths, and continue to learn. If that sounds like someone you know, offer support and recognize their strengths.

THE FIRST PRINCIPLES APPROACH

From building SpaceX to running Tesla, Elon Musk is a controversial innovator. Musk uses a similar line of questioning called "the first principles" approach.

In the first principles approach, you reverse-engineer problems and start with questions like: *What do we know is true? How do we know that?*

"I tend to approach things from a physics framework," Musk said in an interview. "First, we need to boil things down to their fundamental truths. What are we sure is true? Then reason up from there. That takes a lot of mental energy."[15]

The first principles approach is similar to thinking like a scientist because you reflect on your current knowledge and consider other possibilities.

DELIBERATE PRACTICE

Thinking like a scientist is a complex skill that takes time to learn.

In his book *Outliers: The Story of Success*, Malcolm Gladwell proposed it takes ten thousand hours of practice to achieve proficiency in a complex skill.[16] But it is not just about practicing; you need to practice deliberately. Note that ten thousand hours is an arbitrary number and training can accelerate your learning.

Deliberate practice involves considerable, specific, and sustained efforts to do something you cannot do well—or even at all. Even if you fail initially, it does not automatically mean you will not be good at something with practice.

Josh Kaufman, author of *The First 20 Hours: How To Learn Anything Fast*, suggests if you can commit to practicing for at least twenty hours, you can jump over the initial hurdle of frustration and start to see the benefits.[17] Of course, this assumption depends on your abilities and access to resources.

Taking breaks can help when you practice a new skill. Researchers at the National Institutes of Health recorded the brain waves of thirty-three right-handed volunteers. The volunteers were shown the code "41234" on a screen and asked to type it out with their *left* hands as many times as possible for ten seconds and then take a ten second break. They repeated this cycle of alternating practice and rest a total of thirty-five times.

During rest, their brains replayed faster versions of what they just practiced. The results showed that wakeful rest plays just as important a role as practice in learning a new skill.[18]

FAIL TO SUCCEED

Digital agile leaders understand it is possible to gain valuable insights from practicing, failing, and learning. But they do not forgo strategy and reasoning in the name of failing. They use critical thinking, wisdom, and the wisdom of others to anticipate potential issues.

A sense of failure can stem from many things, like getting wrong answers on a test, losing money, making a mistake, or getting rejected or fired. You may have learned that failure is "bad," especially if you were reprimanded for making a mistake or not being "good" at something. But failure is a part of life and how we learn.

It is hard not to take rejection and failure personally. No one likes to fail, at least no one I know. Failures can be costly, resource draining, and downright embarrassing. Yet, being overly risk averse and failure avoidant can be a recipe for disaster. Consider reframing how you view failure and mistakes.

When I joined an innovation team within a company of one thousand employees, the motto was "fail fast." While in principle, *fail fast, fail early, fail forward,* and *fail often* are catchy terms, it is

DIGITAL AGILE LEADER LESSON

Life is not about avoiding mistakes; it is about taking ownership and learning from them.

not about chasing failures. It is about experimenting and aiming for success while also creating space where it is safe to talk about mistakes instead of covering them up. Even when we scrapped an idea, it did not mean it was an outright failure; we were learning, adjusting, and redefining success.

While there are many successes in science, there are also many failures. Failure is how science advances. Rather than being "right," science values discovery. Even after multiple failed attempts, success is still possible.

Take, for example, the story of WD-40. In 1953, in San Diego, the start-up company Rocket Chemical Company developed a line of rust-prevention solvents and degreasers for use in the aerospace industry.

It took them forty attempts to get their formula to work, but on the fortieth attempt, they got it right in a big way. WD-40 Multi-Use Product was born. WD-40 stands for Water Displacement, 40th formula.[19]

Experimentation and determination led to something big. Imagine if you found success on your next try.

DIGITAL AGILE LEADER LESSON
Even after multiple failed attempts, success is still possible.

Bubble Wrap is another example where something can "fail" and still win. In 1957 in New Jersey, engineers Alfred Fielding and Marc Chavannes were trying to create textured wallpaper. They put two pieces of plastic shower curtain through a heat-sealing machine but were disappointed by the results: a sheet of film with trapped air bubbles.

However, they did not totally dismiss their failure. In 1960, they received a patent and founded Sealed Air Corp. The following year they sold Bubble Wrap as packaging material and found success with their first client, IBM.[20]

While Bubble Wrap did not work as wallpaper (although that sounds like a fun idea), it had a widespread application for packaging. Accidental wins are still wins.

DIGITAL AGILE LEADER LESSON

Failure could translate to success somewhere else.
When something goes wrong, it can still go right.

Failure can feel demotivating, but not all failure is bad. When have you experienced failure in your life? What is one thing you learned from that experience? Failure tends to be more past-oriented, and we often tie failure into our sense of self-worth. Reflect and learn from the experience, then consider what you can do moving forward.

INFINITE UNKNOWNS

Scientists are constantly discovering, rediscovering, developing, and refuting theories. The mysteries of our universe are still being unraveled. Not too long ago, we lived in a universe with only a small number of known planets, all of them orbiting our sun. Today, more than five thousand planets are confirmed by NASA space telescopes to exist beyond our solar system.[21]

The irony is the more we learn, the more we realize how little we know. Approaching work and life with this lens can cultivate acceptance that we simply cannot and do not have to know everything.

Our textbooks are playing catch-up to what we unearth every day. If we put that into perspective, it expands our view to an even bigger picture: There are infinite unknowns.

DIGITAL AGILE LEADER LESSON

There are infinite unknowns.
So, we must infinitely unlearn and learn.

The next time you encounter a problem, try thinking like a scientist. This could mean formulating a hypothesis and testing it. It could mean working your way backward from the end goal. It could mean deconstructing long-held beliefs and opening your mind to other possibilities. Or it could simply mean asking more thoughtful questions.

In times of uncertainty, the rules of engagement have changed, and each situation is different. What are your options? You can start by experimenting with a new mindset and exploring the possibilities. Remember, there is a lot we do not see. There is more to the story. And there are infinite unknowns.

TAKEAWAYS AND REFLECTIONS

THINKING LIKE A SCIENTIST MEANS TO REST, TEST, AND LEARN. Try adopting an experimentation mindset. Test ideas in low-risk settings with micro-experiments first, then embolden your plan.

THINKING LIKE A SCIENTIST CAN HELP YOU BREAK DOWN PROBLEMS. Try breaking down problems into more manageable chunks and smaller steps. From there, you can identify alternate pathways and possibilities.

THERE ARE MORE UNKNOWNS THAN KNOWNS. When you practice humility and appreciate how there is so much more to learn, you can adjust your thinking and invite in new ideas.

BALANCE BEING OPEN-MINDED WITH BEING DECISIVE. Consider asking questions like: *What is the problem I am trying to solve? How do I know it is a problem? How big of a problem is it? Even if I do not feel confident, how can I practice making decisions?* With practice, you can gain experience and continue adjusting your sail as the winds change.

CHAPTER 7

CONNECT TO PURPOSE

The noted psychologist Wayne Dyer once said: "When you dance, your purpose is not to get to a certain place on the floor. It's to enjoy each step along the way."

If work were a dance, it probably would not be very graceful. You might stumble along the way, trip over your feet, or call it quits. You might pause to evaluate: *What is the purpose? Why am I here? Am I even making an impact?*

Ultimately, you want to know that you and your efforts matter. You want to feel like there is some worthwhile purpose in whatever you choose to do.

Having a sense of purpose is a fundamental human need. Research has shown that a sense of purpose in life is a powerful predictor of numerous positive outcomes, including stronger immune systems, financial success, and longer life spans.[22]

At some point in your life, you might feel inspired to spend your time more purposefully. This may mean leaving a job to focus on family and other priorities, retiring early, or taking a sabbatical before starting a new chapter.

In a time of reckoning, you may ask existential questions like: *What is the meaning of my being? Who and what do I care about? What will be my legacy?*

CONNECTING TO PURPOSE IN ACTION

Connecting to purpose can feel elusive and out of reach. It certainly felt that way for me in 2016 when I felt stagnant at work. I looked outside the window and watched cars glide over the freeway. One car braked, then another, as if they were interlinked chains responding to changing traffic patterns. I wanted to somehow disrupt my patterns and make a bigger impact. Beyond the four walls of where I worked, I knew there was more to my purpose. When and where would I find it?

If you expect to find your purpose only at work, you may set yourself up for disappointment. No matter how great your job is, there may come a day when you wonder if you should continue down that path. You might be in your role due to societal or familial expectations, but is it aligned with who you are and where you want to go?

I once thought I would find my purpose when I reached a career milestone. I had to unlearn and relearn what purpose and success meant to me. Sometimes, the best way to do that is through conversations with others.

"What does meaningful work mean to you?" I asked Cyrus, a data analytics director.

"What really matters are the people I'm around," said Cyrus. "I could be making widgets for all I care. While that might sound boring, if I'm surrounded by people who inspire me, that is meaningful."

Tracy, a project manager, connects to her purpose by developing others and contributing to their growth. "My job is mundane at times. But I love that I'm activating purpose across my team and helping each person realize how their contributions ladder up to something greater."

Aditya, an HR director, shared, "My purpose is to amplify different voices, build an incredible team and culture, and elevate the employee experience."

Adaku, a hardware engineer, is proud to build innovative products. He smiled as he shared patient stories. "We are saving people's lives, so I inherently feel purposeful. My job gives me purpose. But my primary purpose is being a parent."

Olivia, a sales rep in the professional services industry, enjoys meeting with her clients and learning about their initiatives. "I cherish those momentary, beautiful connections with other people. If I can help my clients solve problems, I feel purposeful. I also want to manage a team, but I'm finding things I like about this role and learning a lot."

Elena, an emergency room doctor, connects to purpose by helping her patients. "I see a lot of heart-wrenching things in the ER. I'm honored if I can use my training to help people. Beyond that, my most purposeful days are with my family."

DEFINING PURPOSE

Purpose can come from multiple sources, including family, community, work, and spirituality. Your purpose can already be within you and be ignited by your efforts and environment.

You can have more than one purpose. Your purpose right now might be to put food on the table, and you may not have the luxury of thinking about the future. Sometimes making it through another day is purposeful enough.

Be mindful of the illusion of purpose. Doing something egregious and calling it "purpose" is fallacious.

PURPOSE SPOTTING

Most leaders agree that cultivating purpose at work and being a purpose-driven company can help attract and retain top talent. One study showed that 79 percent of leaders believe that purpose is central to business success and an organization's existence. Yet only 27 percent of leaders help employees connect their purpose to the work of the company.[23]

As a digital agile leader, you can help your employees connect to purpose by tying their work to the broader mission. It is not just about the company's mission but the employee's *relationship* to that mission. How does the mission resonate with each individual?

Employees also need to take ownership of defining and cultivating purpose. For some employees, purpose means having time for other things outside of work.

"To me, purpose is creating a life outside of work, with a job that gives me flexibility," said Jing. "I can show up, do my job, then find deeper meaning with friends and hobbies."

Flexibility is not just where to work; it is also about working on different projects and with different teams. In addition to flexibility, some employees may want autonomy, variety, or career mobility to feel purposeful.

"My biggest fear is getting too comfortable and complacent and accepting what has been handed to me," Amelia confessed. "I want to keep growing. That is what fuels my purpose."

Jackson had been on the road his entire life as a consultant and found himself between jobs. "My purpose right now is to find stability. I want to get a job that I like, work with people that I like, and earn a decent living."

As a leader, you can create a space where purpose can flourish. Encourage employees to build purpose into their roles and find reasons to be inspired. Learn what each employee values and have meaningful discussions about growth.

It can be helpful to define your Employee Value Proposition (EVP), which includes culture, pay, career development, technology, flexibility, and other unique benefits. Then measure and monitor the effectiveness of your EVP through metrics such as employee satisfaction scores, retention, and referral rates.

FUNDAMENTAL HUMAN NEEDS

You may have heard of Manfred Max-Neef's Fundamental Human Needs. Max-Neef, a Chilean economist, developed a taxonomy based on his work on Human Scale Development. It includes nine human needs: Subsistence, Protection, Affection, Understanding, Participation, Leisure, Creation, Identity, and Freedom. For each need, there are four existential categories: Being, Having, Doing, and Interacting. Together, these make up a thirty-six-cell matrix that defines fundamental human needs.[24]

Let's look at existential categories across the Identity need. *Being* could mean having a sense of belonging; *Having* identity could be via religion, language, and culture; *Doing* includes getting to know yourself; and *Integrating* your identity can be done via social settings.

Max-Neef stressed that needs are not absolute and can differ across cultures. He also notes that *satisfiers* are different from needs. For example, a house is not a need, but a way to satisfy the need for *subsistence.*

Employers cannot satisfy every need, so the idea is to become more self-sufficient.

A DIFFERENT TAKE ON MASLOW'S HIERARCHY OF NEEDS

You may also be familiar with Maslow's Hierarchy[25] which illustrates five levels of human needs in a pyramid. These needs range from basic physiological needs (air, water, food) to safety (security, employment), love and belonging (relationships, connection), esteem (respect, recognition), and self-actualization.

One of the flaws with this approach is the assumption that our needs are hierarchical. Up to a point, our basic needs have to be satisfied. Beyond that, the sequence and extent of needs satisfaction is up to individuals. We can have multiple needs exist simultaneously.

Relationships and power dynamics also come into play. For instance, we may risk basic needs, such as sleep, to find a job—sometimes not for our own sake but for our children.[26]

MASLOW'S HIERARCHY OF NEEDS

SELF-ACTUALIZATION
Desire to become the most that one can be

ESTEEM
Respect, self-esteem, status, recognition, strength, freedom

LOVE AND BELONGING
Friendship, intimacy, family, sense of connection

SAFETY NEEDS
Personal security, employment, resources, health, property

PHYSIOLOGICAL NEEDS
Air, water, food, shelter, sleep, clothing

Despite its flaws, this model is still useful for understanding human behavior. At the basic level, this means providing fair compensation and a good working environment for your employees. Beyond that, learn what matters specifically to them.

MAKE THE CONNECTION

Ask your employees. What matters to you? How do you like to create impact? Is it by training people, solving problems, or defining and streamlining processes? Check individual purpose against the broader purpose. This can evolve over time.

Give them opportunities. Create opportunities for employees and elevate their visibility. Encourage them to showcase their work through speaking, writing, or other avenues. Find ways to engage them in different projects so they can develop their skills.

Help them set goals. Discuss specific goals and action steps. What do they need to do to achieve a goal? How can you help?

Remind them of the bigger picture. Uncover ways people might want to be altruistic and provide acts of service.

You can help your employees connect to purpose by asking the below questions:

ORGANIZATIONAL PURPOSE	INDIVIDUAL PURPOSE
What does our organization do? Why is that important? *(Review organizational goals)*	Why do you think your role is important? How is it meaningful to you?
How do we provide value? What impact do we make?	How do you provide value? What are your biggest strengths?
How do we give back to the community?	How do you want to give back to the community?
Why does our team exist? *(Reaffirm the purpose of the team)*	What do you think the team's purpose is? How do you relate to it?

You can also ask:

- Do you feel your work matters? Why or why not?
- Can you see your contributions?
- How do your contributions connect to the organization's broader mission?
- How do you want to create an impact outside of the organization?

CHECK IN WITH YOURSELF

Think about your relationship with work. What does work mean to you? Just a paycheck? A place where you can develop your skills and make a difference? When does time seem to fly by? What energizes or drains you?

Can you find purpose in your job? There may be parts of the job you do not like, but also parts that are meaningful. See if you can find and build meaningful work where you are.

If you are unsure of your purpose, try these exercises:

- Reflect on your life and try to uncover key themes. Why did you choose a certain path?
- What do you wish you could do more of? Less of?
- What are you good at?
- Think about the obstacles you have faced. When were you brave, either by choice or because you had to be? What does that tell you about yourself?

- Where are you unsatisfied? How might the pain drive you to transform your life?

- Think about what is going on in the world. What issues bother you? Where do you want to make an impact?

- What problems have you solved? What problems do you *want* to solve? Why is that important to you?

- Verbalize and write down your goals. Start with a five- to ten-minute visualization primer. Try to envision details about where you are, who you are with, and what you are doing.

- What daily habits might interfere with your goals? If your goal is to be more present in your relationships and you have a habit of checking your phone every five minutes, consider putting your phone out of reach or turning off notifications. Practice self-compassion and patience as you modify your habits and align with your goals.

- Simplify purpose. It could be as simple as spending time with family or helping a friend.

Rather than waiting for your purpose, go out there and create it. Find inspiration through experiences and conversations.

UNCOVER THEMES

Your purpose and values can change over time. Think about what you used to want and how that might have changed over the years. What matters to you now?

I USED TO WANT	NOW I WANT	INSIGHT
Independence	Independence	Independence is still something I value.
To travel the world	To buy a house	Stability is more important than adventure at this time in my life.
A job that pays well	A job with flexibility or a short commute	I am willing to take a salary cut because it is important to be near my family.
To go back to school	To make more money	My financial situation has changed, and I need to earn more money.
A promotion	Time for self-care	Throughout my career, my self-care has taken a back seat. I need to prioritize my well-being right now.
Socializing on weekends	Time for myself	I used to say yes to social outings. Now I prefer spending time on other hobbies.
Building my career	Building a family	I spent decades developing my career. Now I want to focus on other areas of my life, including building a family.

This exercise highlights how your values and purpose may have shifted over time.

John, a global sales executive, realized his purpose had shifted significantly in the last decade. He would travel so often for work that sometimes he would forget where he was.

"I had to call the hotel front desk and ask them what city I was in. That was before all this technology. No joke," he said with a straight face. "On top of that, I was exhausted. At that moment I realized I was ready to quit."

John worked for a few more years before retiring, or "redirecting my sail," as he preferred to say. "Now, my purpose has completely changed. I am working on several projects that keep me busy and I have a bucket list with over forty items. I am still active, but my days look different. When it comes to my career, I have forgotten a lot. What I *do* remember and cherish are the people and experiences. They still fuel my purpose."

CREATE YOUR "I AM" STATEMENT

If you are unsure about your next step or how to derive purpose, you can try creating an "I am" statement. I developed this exercise for my clients and use it regularly. This statement includes who you are and what you like to do. Below are some examples.

- I am an empathetic and innovative teacher. My mission in life is to transform the lives of students through education.

- I am an experienced healthcare leader, passionate about solving complex problems. My mission is to improve the lives of patients around the world.

- I am a parent. My mission is to empower my children and give them the tools to thrive in the world.

Start by writing "I am," and think about a few words that describe who you are. You do not have to commit to a purpose; just consider one of several possibilities. Be mindful of dysfunctional beliefs that come up and challenge them when they do.

LIMITING BELIEF	CHALLENGE BACK STATEMENT
I need to find my purpose ASAP.	There is no standard timeline. I will do my best and put in the effort. That is purposeful.
I should know what I want to do.	It is okay not to have all the answers. I can talk to others and think about what I want.
I will never figure it out.	I will keep exploring, asking questions, and trying new things. From there I will decide my next steps.
I am too <fill in the blank> to achieve what I want.	I am resourceful and can figure it out. Some of my strengths include: _____
I am falling behind other people who appear further ahead in life.	I do not know everyone's full story. I am doing my best and will be kind to myself. I will reach out to others and seek support.

IKIGAI

Ikigai is a Japanese philosophy that means *reason for being*.[27] The concept of Ikigai suggests that our emotional, mental, and physical states are affected by our sense of purpose. Ikigai can help you identify what to do with your life by evaluating these four dimensions:

· What you love

· What you are good at

· What you can get paid for

· What the world needs

It can be challenging to find something that satisfies all four circles in the Ikigai framework. You might be good at something you do not love. Your interests can also change as you try new things and learn new skills.

The reality is you can find fulfillment in various activities and roles. Still, it might be helpful to look at this framework as you weigh your options. Think about your Ikigai as your (current) North Star and what you aspire to do or try.

Be mindful when searching for something perfect delays you from taking action. When an opportunity comes your way, consider it—even if it is not ideal. Remember, it does not have to be forever. Get your foot in the door, learn, then adjust.

The truth is work may not always be fun or easy, and persistence can go a long way. Sometimes the purpose is embedded in staying the course and learning as you go.

DIGITAL AGILE LEADER LESSON
Sometimes the purpose is (in) the process.

START WITH A STEP

If it feels like you are experiencing stagnation day after day, deeply unsatisfied and longing for more, remember that life can change on a dime. View stagnancy as a signal that something new awaits you. You may have to ignite change by taking the first step.

The first step can be so small and barely visible. Perhaps it is just a thought: *What if…?* What if you changed your perspective? What if you could find new ways to get inspired? What if you developed a healthier relationship with yourself? With others? With your expectations? What if you gave yourself permission to rest and reevaluate?

Start with a thought. That thought can become stronger until you are motivated to take action, even if it is one step or micro-movement. Allow those steps to build on each other, and before you know it, you will be paving a more purposeful path.

What are you waiting for? And remember, simply being *is* purposeful.

TAKEAWAYS AND REFLECTIONS

PURPOSE CAN EVOLVE AND BE MORE THAN ONE. Your purpose today might be to survive and put food on the table. A year from today, it could be something else.

EMPOWER YOUR EMPLOYEES TO CONNECT TO PURPOSE. Learn how each person on your team relates to their work and how they might want to make work more meaningful. Help them connect their purpose to the broader mission and remind them of their value.

CONNECT TO YOUR PURPOSE. What does work mean to you? What are some things you might want to explore? How do you define purpose and integrate it into your life?

GO BEYOND THE WORKPLACE. Work is one of many places to connect to your purpose. Examine who you are across other dimensions. Who are you when you are with others? When you are alone?

REFLECT ON YOUR HABITS AND GOALS. How are your habits interfering with your goals? What daily habits do you want to modify? If you want to sleep earlier, establish a routine or ritual that signals the end of the day, like reading a book or putting away your work.

CREATE PURPOSE. In a world where you might question, *What is it all for? Why am I here?* purpose becomes an anchor that holds you steady if you drift away at sea. Build purpose by starting somewhere and putting in the effort. Evaluate what you want and your priorities. Get out of your own way. Have the conversation, go to the event, say yes to an opportunity, and allow yourself to dream.

CONSIDER INDIVIDUALISTIC AND COLLECTIVE PURPOSE. Your purpose can be to provide for your family as well as for the greater good.

STEP OUTSIDE YOURSELF. Sometimes you may get trapped in your head, and the best way to feel purposeful is to help someone else.

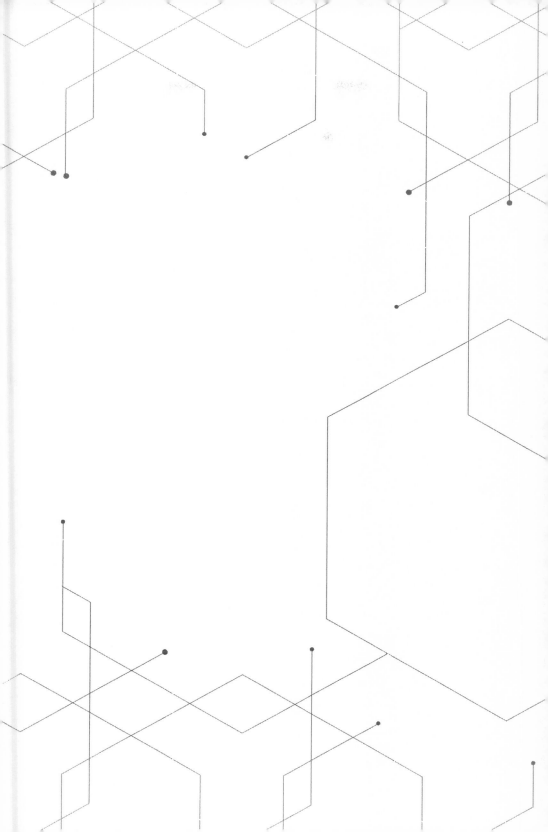

CHAPTER 8

CO-CREATE CAREER PATHS

When Ethan threw his phone on the table in an explosive outburst, I winced in my seat as the sound reverberated through the walls. Ethan was a tall, silver-haired senior partner with a booming voice, flush cheeks, and smile that lit up the room. Only that day, he was not smiling. Tensions were high, milestones were approaching, and we had to deliver the project's next phase.

"Just get it *done!*" He stormed out of the room and slammed the door behind him.

"Do you want to be a partner at the firm?" Ethan asked me later that evening at our team dinner. His beaming smile was back.

Not after what I saw earlier today.

"Yes," I responded. It was a knee-jerk reaction. That was what I thought I *should* want. I did not fully know what partnership entailed, other than this elusive destination. It surely was desirable to be a partner. Who would not want the lofty title and perks?

Yet only a small percentage of consultants become partner and they must make tradeoffs along the way. Once at the top of the ladder, partners may find themselves at the bottom rung of another ladder with more senior partners above them. I admired those who reached the destination but questioned if it was for me.

Traditional up-or-out career paths did not work for everyone. To retain talent, the firm also had a "specialist" path for people who wanted to deliver great work without the added pressure of vying for partner. This helped with retention, and many consultants chose this alternate path. With only two tracks available, however, the options for growth seemed limited.

"Partnership is a highly selective process," he explained. "You need to increase the size of the pie and bring in revenue. I think you are partner material."

I was flattered and certain that would be my career path. I was set and had it figured out.

Or so I thought.

While I was ambitious, the road to becoming a partner was long and arduous for various reasons.

Regardless, I had to shift focus to my declining health and take a leave of absence. My doctor told me, "Your career may be hitting a plateau, but that does not mean it's over. Use this plateau to heal and recover."

Although it took a while for me to climb out of each plateau and valley, I persevered. I could not have done it without the support of others. I learned to embrace the plateaus and view them as opportunities to reflect and reset.

What are some valleys you have hit on your journey? How did you climb out and move forward?

You may admire the upper echelon and desire to reach a similar status within an organization. You might think that is what you *should* want. But you can spend years trying to inch your way up a ladder you cannot see. And once you do, the goalposts might change.

In addition, you could compromise your health and values in the name of achievement. There may be other options better suited for your situation.

THE GAME OF LIFE

In the original The Game of Life board game, the career choices were doctor, journalist, teacher, lawyer, and physicist. We have come a long way since then, thankfully.

Today, there are countless ways to earn a living. There are infinite, nonlinear paths that are unique to everyone. No one path is better than the other; they are all meaningful. As I reflect on my path, I remember the highs and lows, stops, starts, obstacles, sharp turns, and detours (and it is not over yet).

Today's career path is not about the *climb*; it is about *customization*. I used to chase the climb until I realized it was an endless staircase. If you customize your career and allow it to take different shapes, you can find fulfillment in unexpected ways.

DIGITAL AGILE LEADER LESSON
*Career paths are less about the climb
and more about the customization.*

WHAT DO YOU WANT?

What do you want?

Have you ever been asked that question? How did it feel?

Leo, my former manager, asked me that during a career conversation. At that moment, it felt like he was asking me to solve a highly complicated physics problem. I sat there like a deer in headlights and furrowed my brow.

The truth was, I did not know. Or at least, I could not articulate what I wanted. What were my options? Where could I go next? Did I have to pick just one thing? Could I change my mind? I felt stuck, and career conversations left me more stressed and confused.

I had to go inward and reflect on what I wanted. It was not a title. It was a *feeling*. I wanted to feel like I was valued and appreciated. I wanted to make an impact and grow. I had different interests like technology, education, and solving problems. But I could not fit that description neatly into a title or role. Besides, how could I move forward when I kept hitting obstacles?

Obstacles like exclusion or hostile working environments can impact how far you go. Internal barriers like attitudes and beliefs can also get in the way. It is important to identify internal and external barriers and address the underlying cause.

Sometimes it is tough to pinpoint what you want. Consider asking the following questions:

· What do you want to *try next*?

· What are some skills you want to develop?

· What projects or subject areas interest you? Why?

- What is something you think about doing, even though it seems difficult?

- What internal and external barriers are you facing? How do they impact your ability to achieve your goals?

Get creative and work with your employees to define a career path that can be multidirectional, not just linear and upward. Identify how the environment might be hindering or helping them.

PROVIDE A PATH

A job title is only one piece of information that describes who you are and what you do. You can be multiple things at once—a leader, teacher, parent, mentor, and student. At different phases of your life you may want different things, which is normal. You may prefer to gain experience over titles, and skills over pay. Or you may want to fast-track your career.

Some employees may prioritize stability over career growth. Others may want variety and challenge. Everyone has unique gifts and goals, and we need all kinds of people to make work *work*.

Take Tina, for example. Tina was a reliable and loyal employee in the defense industry who excelled in her role as systems analyst. Her manager, Peter, believed she would be the best person to lead the team as it grew. When he gave her additional leadership responsibilities, however, Tina protested.

"I don't want to manage *anyone*," she said. "I love what I do." Tina wanted to work on cutting-edge projects, not lead people.

Peter eventually hired another manager, and Tina was thrilled to focus on advancing her technical skills.

Ben could always count on his executive assistant, Gerri, and genuinely appreciated her. He told everyone, "Gerri is the best executive assistant."

Gerri was grateful at first but over time felt deflated. "Ben has only known me in that capacity. I can do more. I think he means well, but I don't like being limited and labeled. In fact, I'd like to move into another role at some point, but I'm not sure if he'd support that."

THE CAREER PATH CONVERSATION

Employees also need to take ownership of their careers and establish credibility. This includes taking initiative, setting goals, and building relationships.

Sometimes barriers can block those efforts. Consider if you or someone else might intentionally or unintentionally make it difficult for certain individuals (or anyone) to advance. Examine your limiting beliefs about success.

You might be holding on to good talent, but that will not win their hearts nor loyalty. How can you create more meaningful career paths for your employees, even if that means they leave?

When you have a career path conversation, it is important to get into the right frame of mind and set your intentions. Why are you having the conversation? Is it to check the box? Or are you genuinely interested in your employees' growth?

To have a more productive career conversation:

Be transparent. Do not make promises you cannot keep. Without transparency, people may fill in the gaps and create their narratives.

Be flexible. Build flexibility into the plan as people's goals and business priorities might shift.

Connect with consistency. Do not have twice-a-year conversations; follow up and follow through consistently.

Understand yourself. Examine your perspectives. Talk to people who can respectfully challenge any limiting beliefs and blind spots.

Understand the individual. Beyond curiosity, have *empathetic curiosity.* This means learning what someone wants and why it matters *to them specifically.*

Collaborate. Work with employees to outline the desired skills and goals. Invite them to share their ideas.

Give access to opportunities. Provide opportunities for learning and development, including access to mentors. While mentors generally give career advice, sponsors open doors and advocate for employees. Encourage employees to build their reputation and find support inside and outside the organization. Consider how you can bridge any accessibility gaps.

Shift your focus to building your team's capabilities. Find ways employees can make an impact—even if that means letting go of work you want to do.

Co-create career paths by inviting your employees to the conversation and allowing them to take an active role. A career conversation might include asking these questions:

- What do you like and not like about your current role?
- What keeps you engaged? What demotivates you?
- If you could create any role at the company, what would it be?
- How would that tie into your goals? Into the company's goals?
- How can you develop your network?
- How do you want to build your brand and skills inside and outside the company?

To wrap up the conversation, you can say:

- What are some key takeaways before we wrap up?
- How do you feel about the plan so far, and what might you need from me?

While you cannot guarantee a new role or promotion, you can help employees find development opportunities. Sometimes what they need most is confidence in their abilities.

You may not be able to retain every employee. But it is not just about retention; it is also about cultivating respectful relationships and your leadership legacy. If an employee decides to leave, they will remember how you treated them, and ideally it would be a good memory. Former employees can boomerang back. They can also become brand ambassadors, vendors, or clients. You never know how paths will intersect again in the future.

EVALUATE THE ARCHITECTURE

It is also a good idea to evaluate your talent architecture. How are your teams structured?

Based on how you architect your team, career growth can feel limited. For example, an engineer that reports into the Project Management Office might want a more technical career path.

Additionally, when there are leadership changes, employees need to reset expectations. This could create stress for employees, and they may get lost in the shuffle.

GET TO KNOW YOURSELF

Think about your path. Perhaps you have worked your way to your current position or have been in the same role for several years. Maybe you encountered certain barriers along the way. How did you move around or through those barriers? How can you modify barriers for others?

When chasing your purpose becomes an obsession and you cannot sit still:

- Take a moment to breathe.
- Try not to put so much pressure on yourself.
- Do what you can and allow things to unfold.
- Consider making a decision now and pivoting later.
- Get to know who you are and reflect on your goals.
- Be mindful when self-reflection leads to self-importance, and you forget to bring others along.

So, what do you want?

TAKEAWAYS AND REFLECTIONS

COMPENSATION CAN ONLY GO SO FAR. Companies need to look at multiple ways to retain talent, including crafting custom career paths.

CO-CREATING CAREER PATHS MEANS HAVING REGULAR CONVERSATIONS WITH EMPLOYEES AND CREATING TANGIBLE ACTION STEPS. Both parties need to put in the effort to identify possible paths. Explore long-term career aspirations and not just the next step.

ASK EMPLOYEES DIRECTLY WHAT THEY CARE ABOUT. Sometimes people do not know what they want. Still, have the conversation to encourage thinking, planning, and accountability.

THINK ABOUT YOUR CAREER PATH. Spend time reflecting on your goals and strengths. Take ownership of your career by initiating conversations with your managers and mentors. If those efforts do not lead anywhere, consider your next steps and where else you can get support.

EVALUATE YOUR RELATIONSHIP TO YOUR CAREER. How emotionally invested are you in your career? Putting undue pressure on yourself to succeed could cause stress and burnout. Consider how you want to integrate other parts of your life.

EMBRACE JAGGED PATHS. Career paths are not always linear, upward, and continuous. There may be pivots and pauses in between. It is easy to get caught up in the comparison game. But that can be misleading and create more anxiety. Everyone's path is unique.

OPTIMIZE TEAM STRUCTURE. Evaluate the talent architecture and how teams are structured. What is working and what is not? There may be opportunities to enhance efficiency and career growth.

REVIEW BARRIERS AND OPPORTUNITIES. Some people may face barriers along their path. These barriers can be overt or subtle. Consider how you can build more inclusive spaces and break down barriers. While this is a collective effort, it also makes a difference at the individual level.

CHAPTER 9

AMPLIFY YOUR EI
(EMOTIONAL INTELLIGENCE)

"If you aren't falling down, you aren't trying hard enough," my skating coach shouted from across the rink.

So, I fell. A lot.

I took up figure skating in my early twenties after going to our local ice rink with some friends. As I clung tightly to the wall and inched my way timidly around the rink, my friends whizzed past me.

Learning to skate requires self-awareness, a key component of emotional intelligence. I was self-aware enough to know I was a terrible skater, so I enrolled in lessons. While I ultimately hung up my skates, I learned a lot during that time.

Skating requires complete focus the moment you step onto the rink. My worries would melt away into the ice as I was abruptly awakened to the present moment. I had to pay close attention to my form and the position of my blades. One minor misstep and I would lose balance. It was focus or fall.

One morning while practicing my axel jump, I carved the blades into the ice and gradually increased my speed. I set up the jump, got into position, and then nothing.

I backed out.

Over time, I made bolder moves (well, bold for me, anyway). I became more confident with practice and less fearful of falling. That does not mean the falls did not hurt. It meant I was not always anticipating and thinking, *I am going to fall any minute now.*

When I missed a jump or nearly collided with another skater, I was frustrated. I felt a range of emotions as I faced new challenges. I was new to this emotional intelligence stuff, and it would take some work.

DEFINING EMOTIONAL INTELLIGENCE

Emotional intelligence (which I will refer to as EI or EQ interchangeably) is capacity of an individual to see, understand, and manage their emotions. You can think of emotions as energy in motion or energy moving through the body. The roots for motion and emotion are nearly identical. *Movere*, in Latin, means to move. *Exmovere* or *emovere* means to move out, so emotions "move" something inside of us.[28]

The words *emotional intelligence* ironically might conjure mixed emotions for you. You might be skeptical and ask: does emotional intelligence really exist? Can it be measured? Does every job require EI? What about an artist or machinist who creates parts with a high degree of precision? Or a surgeon who performs emergency surgery to save a life? How much EI do they need?

These are good questions, and we have much to learn about the science of emotions. The concepts within emotional intelligence are still valuable if you want to be more self-aware. The word *intelligence* implies that you not only have awareness; you do something about that awareness and regulate your emotions.

FUTURE SKILLS

The World Economic Forum[29] identified specific skills needed in 2025 and beyond, listed in alphabetical order below.

- Active learning and learning strategies
- Analytical thinking and innovation
- Complex problem-solving
- Creativity, originality, and initiative
- Critical thinking and analysis
- Emotional intelligence
- Leadership and social influence
- Persuasion and negotiation
- Reasoning, problem-solving, and ideation
- Resilience, stress tolerance, and flexibility
- Service orientation
- Systems analysis and evaluation
- Technology design and programming
- Technology use, monitoring, and control
- Troubleshooting and user experience

People-centric skills will continue to be in demand, including emotional intelligence. Whether artificial intelligence becomes advanced enough to replicate these skills remains to be seen. As humans, we can develop and leverage these important skills.

Emotional intelligence can be viewed across two dimensions: *self* and *social*. You can learn to recognize and regulate your emotions and extend empathy to others.

	RECOGNIZE	REGULATE
SELF	Awareness	Self-management
SOCIAL	Empathy	Relationship management

While there are several assessments that are helpful for reflection and discussion, emotional intelligence is hard to measure. In one study, emotional intelligence scores declined as leaders advanced above middle management, with CEOs having the lowest EQs in the workplace, on average.[30]

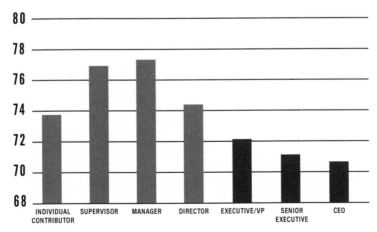

EMOTIONAL INTELLIGENCE AND JOB TITLE

That is not because CEOs do not care. At that level, leaders need to make difficult business decisions and appease shareholders. Some CEOs may have attained their position due to their technical prowess and developing EI was not a priority.

AMPLIFY YOUR EI

Take Damian, for example. He was a creative and passionate entrepreneur with a team of trusted colleagues, including his long-term friend, Ericka, a senior technology leader. The team was about to launch a revolutionary product that would disrupt the industry.

After a team meeting, Ericka was speechless. Damian had just berated her in front of her colleagues for something that was not her fault. The product launch was delayed, and she worked fervently behind the scenes to get things back on track. Why did Damian humiliate her like that?

After a private cry, she composed a message and then edited it (observe the strikethroughs):

> ~~Dear~~ Damian,
>
> I'm surprised by your behavior today. ~~You were a complete jerk.~~ You were out of line when you yelled at me in front of everyone. Do you realize how that made me feel? ~~I hate you, you *&·^%@ !%$%# piece of *$#%~~
>
> Please accept this letter as my resignation. My last day will be August 6th.

> ~~Sincerely, Regards,~~
> *Ericka*
> *PS: Good luck with everything.*

Ericka fought back tears as her finger hovered over the "send" button. After a few minutes of deliberating, she slammed her laptop shut and went home.

Ericka could have responded in several ways. She could have resigned, yelled back at Damian, sought revenge, asked for help, reported the issue, or walked away. She chose to walk away and contemplated quitting her job.

What would you have done in that situation?

The next morning, Ericka had a change of heart and a change of plan. She decided it would be best to confront Damian. They had known each other for over a decade and his behavior seemed out of character. Ericka knew that if she had tried to reason with him during his outburst, it would have been counterproductive. Besides, she was so caught off guard that she could not think straight.

Delaying her reaction had an unexpected benefit. It allowed her to collect her thoughts and think about her next steps. Ericka took a deep breath and picked up the phone. By then, Damian had also regrouped and felt remorseful about how he acted.

"I'd like to talk about yesterday," Ericka said assertively and calmly. She had practiced in front of the mirror a few times that morning. Her heart was racing, but her voice held steady.

"Yes, of course," Damian said. "First and foremost, I want to apologize. That was out of character and out of line."

Ericka was pleased to see how quickly he admitted wrongdoing. But she was not ready to let him off the hook just yet. "It *was* out of line. To be honest, I felt humiliated." She anxiously crumpled up a piece of paper in her hands.

"Rightfully so. I am sorry, and it won't happen again." Damian glanced at a photo of his family. He knew he had to tame his temper, otherwise, he would lose his reputation and a valuable employee.

Ericka let several seconds pass and silence infused the atmosphere. "Are you okay?" she finally asked. That was a million-dollar question. No one had asked Damian that in a while. He had not even asked himself.

"I'm not sure. But I will be. More importantly, are *you* okay? And are we?" Damian knew he was not perfect, but he was no monster either.

Ericka knew she had to forgive Damian, otherwise it would be challenging to continue working there. But she also knew things had to change. Over the next few months, they had more candid conversations. Ericka grew confident in her ability to stand up for herself and others.

Relationships can be repaired, even after a setback or outburst. It takes courage, forgiveness, accountability, action, and a desire for both parties to move forward. Everyone has different thresholds, and some relationships may be severed permanently. Sometimes that might be in the best interest of both parties and it is time to move on.

PUT IN THE EFFORT

A few weeks later, I met Damian at a conference. We explored what was getting in his way and how he was sabotaging his relationships.

In addition to seeing a therapist, Damian met with me for several coaching sessions. At the end of our engagement, he turned to me and said, "For the first time in a long time, I feel heard and seen. You didn't judge me; you made me feel safe."

"Imagine if your team said the same thing to you. If they also felt heard and seen. Imagine what you could accomplish together."

Damian smiled and nodded in agreement.

UNDERSTAND YOUR OPTIONS

During his outburst, Damian experienced an amygdala hijack, a normal and automatic response when emotions take over. When your amygdala gets hijacked, you can get swept into an emotional spiral, making it hard to think logically. In the interest of self-preservation, you might fight back, flee from the scene, or freeze in place.

When our ancestors faced dangers in the wild, they had to react to survive. We still have these primordial instincts, and it takes conscious effort to rewire our programming. The goal is not to silence your negative emotions. This can breed resentment and *toxic positivity*, which means putting a positive spin on even profoundly tragic experiences.[31] Allow yourself to feel your emotions rather than maintain an unrealistic and dangerous façade of positivity.

Keep in mind the human brain is wired for negative thinking, not happiness. We tend to imagine dangers, ruminate about the past, worry about what others think, and not feel good enough.[32] You might replay events in your mind and focus more on negative feedback than on praise. This is known as the *negativity bias.* While a negativity bias is normal and even helpful sometimes, it can also get in the way.

Where in your life have you been too hard on yourself? How can you cut yourself some slack and recognize your efforts? When do your emotions help you or hold you back?

Emotions serve a purpose and there are no "good" or "bad" emotions. Frustration can motivate you to act. Anger can help you fight for justice. But if anger is used as the main activator, it can be draining and deter potential allies. Additionally, anger is usually accompanied by other emotions like fear, disappointment, or hurt. What else is going on beneath the veil of anger? The key is to be aware of your emotions and how they help or hurt you (and others).

APPLY A CULTURAL LENS

Some psychologists believe our current understanding of emotional intelligence is incomplete, and *culture-specific* emotional intelligence is driven by cultural values.[33] European American parents, for example, tend to put the focus on the child's feelings, whereas East-Asian American parents may prefer to emphasize their children's relatedness to others and social norms.[34]

In addition, suppressing emotions has been found to have negative psychological and social consequences in Western cultural contexts. Yet, in other cultural contexts, emotion suppression is less likely to have negative consequences.[35]

There are also nuances within subpopulations. For example, due to societal stressors, some Black Americans may operate with caution when expressing their emotions due to the fear of being negatively evaluated by others.[36]

We cannot assume one worldview since there are differences across cultures and individuals. Emotions are complex. It is important to understand an individual's unique lived experiences and apply a cultural lens to EQ. Imposing a general construct on someone could lead to inaccurate interpretations.

CULTURAL HUMILITY

Cultural intelligence (CQ) is a key extension of EQ. Cultural intelligence is related to emotional intelligence, but it picks up where emotional intelligence leaves off.[37] While emotions are a shared human experience, CQ honors emotional diversity.

There are four components to CQ, including:

- **Drive (motivational):** The interest and ability to learn about new cultures.

- **Knowledge (cognitive):** Understanding how cultures are similar and different and how they influence what people say and do.

- **Strategy (metacognitive):** Respecting cultural differences and checking your assumptions.

· **Action (behavioral):** Adapting your behaviors to include different cultures.[38]

Cultural humility, a different but related concept, is based on a life-long dedication to learning. It means learning about other people's experiences, while being aware of your embeddedness in culture(s).[39] With cultural humility, you accept not knowing everything and develop a mindset of curiosity.

Remember, each person has unique lived experiences and perspectives, regardless of their background. We do not want to reinforce stereotypes, assume a monolithic outlook, or perpetuate an "us versus them" mindset. Instead, remain curious and open to learning.

LISTEN TO OTHERS

Even within families, there can be cultural differences.

To illustrate, one evening my mom and I disagreed on a particular issue. After hitting an impasse, I paused to think about what she said. English is not her first language, and my Hindi is atrocious. Perhaps we misunderstood one another. I soon realized we agreed on several points but came at it from different angles and used different words.

I remember thinking, *She doesn't get it; what is she talking about?* Once I shut up and listened, I realized she was right. I missed out by not paying attention and remaining curious.

We cannot assume what someone is thinking or feeling; we need to ask and clarify. While naming your emotions can help you pinpoint what you are feeling, emotional vocabulary does not translate precisely across cultures. For instance, the words *shame* and *guilt* exist in other languages, but the valuations and expressions can differ across cultural contexts.

Facial expressions and nonverbal cues are also not universal. A perceived look of confusion can be contemplation. A bout of indigestion might be mistaken as disappointment.

Sometimes it is hard to express what is on our hearts. It can be difficult to find the right words to say and descriptors to use for our emotions in *any* language, especially when we are triggered. Our speech and language processing rate can vary, so active listening is important. Active listening includes clarifying what you hear and being present in the conversation.

LISTEN TO YOUR BODY

It is important to also listen to your body. Our bodies are constantly sending us signals. How do your emotions physically manifest? Perhaps fear shows up as a clenched jaw or nervous stomach. Pay attention to these signals so you are aware when you are triggered. Awareness is key to developing emotional intelligence.

Coping mechanisms such as breathing, listening to music, taking a break, exercising, or talking to someone are some ways to regulate your emotions. When you are triggered, however, it can be challenging to employ these strategies. Try a few and see what works for you in different situations.

Note that coping mechanisms vary across cultures. For example, certain cultural rituals and traditions can provide relief from emotional stress. When you Amplify Your EI, you understand there are multiple ways to express and regulate emotions.

UNDERSTAND YOUR TRIGGERS

The first step to Amplify Your EI is to recognize your emotions are there for a reason and you are not alone.

It is important to get to the root cause of *why* you are feeling and behaving a certain way. When was the last time you were frustrated or upset? What triggered you? Was it because you felt ignored or dismissed? Manipulated or misunderstood? Lied to or excluded? Betrayed or interrupted?

- What are your top three triggers? Why?
- What do you typically do when you are triggered?

Your well-being can also impact your emotional intelligence. Perhaps you reacted a certain way due to stress, lack of sleep, or hunger. Or you were frustrated with a situation but lashed out at a person.

Keep in mind, emotions are contagious. Instinctively, we tend to align with the emotions we perceive during interactions. When someone smiles at you, you might smile back to align with the other person's emotion.[40] Likewise, if someone complains, you might join in.

When you think about how interconnected we all are, you can see how your emotions influence people around you. This does not mean you should use emotional intelligence to manipulate others for personal gain. That is what narcissists do. Instead develop authentic EQ. Authentic EQ involves accountability, empathy for others, and self-awareness.[41]

NEURODIVERSITY AND EI

Psychologists continue to research emotional intelligence and have observed that it lies on a continuum with logical intelligence at the other end.[42] In other words, some people are governed by emotions while others are more logical. Each of us falls somewhere along a bell curve of cognitive processes and mental skills, just as with most human traits.[43]

Neurodiversity therefore is a key consideration. Some people may find it difficult to recognize and express their emotions. Rather than stigmatize neurodiversity and categorize it as a "disorder," think about EI skills existing on a continuum and celebrate how neurodiverse we are.

We all have different strengths and being different is not defective. Leaders can challenge misconceptions and empower neurodivergent employees to reach their potential.

CHOOSE YOUR BATTLES

It can be challenging to express your emotions and feel understood. You might feel obligated to be a role model and stay calm under pressure; otherwise, you risk being labeled as emotional, volatile, or reactive.

Perhaps you overmonitor your emotions in attempt to change perceptions. This can be daunting work that you should not have to take on yourself. It can lead to a vicious cycle and shielding yourself more, leaving you depleted. The cycle looks like this:

· You are not frustrated but someone assumes you are.

· You try to express how you feel.

· You feel misunderstood or judged for how you expressed yourself, which leads to frustration.

DIGITAL AGILE LEADER LESSON

The best way to break the cycle is to become more adept at emotional intelligence.

This is a frustrating cycle and sometimes you may want to "win." In some cases, "winning" means walking away. It may not be your fight to fight, and it might be better to enlist support. Decide if the fight is worth it and if it is the sword you want to fall on.

It can be helpful to articulate what you need and how you want to be addressed. When you speak up and assert yourself, you can build confidence and draw healthy boundaries. Start by experimenting in safe spaces with people you trust.

Remember, just because you are developing heightened self-awareness does not mean everyone is in the same place. You might need to accept where people are.

Dealing with someone with perceived lower EQ can be frustrating. Ironically, your EQ can get tested, turning the mirror back to you. Give people the benefit of the doubt. You never know what someone else is going through. What is within your control and where do you want to invest your energy?

EMOTIONAL LABOR

Emotional intelligence is the ability to understand and manage your emotions. It plays a key role in the process of *emotional labor*, a concept popularized in 1983 by American professor Arlie Hochschild.

Emotional labor is using emotive skills to fulfill the emotional requirements of a job. Jobs that require emotional labor include sales, hospitality, and healthcare. For example, if you are in a customer-facing role, you might be expected to keep customers happy. Perhaps you are in a bad mood, and you still need to have a friendly attitude with customers.

There are two components of emotional labor: surface acting and deep acting. In surface acting, you display the required emotions without changing how you actually feel. With deep acting, you change your internal feelings to align with expectations, producing more genuine emotional displays.[44]

Emotional labor, like physical labor, can be tiring when done repeatedly all day long. When there is a discrepancy between what you feel and how you "should" act, it is exhausting to maintain a front. Take breaks and connect with people on a genuine level to reduce the strain of acting.

BEYOND A BUZZWORD

Beyond a buzzword, emotional intelligence helps you build self-awareness and invite people in rather than push them away.

It is possible to be empathetic while being assertive and holding people accountable. Create space for people to share and acknowledge their feelings. Offer support then refocus the conversation.

While emotional intelligence may not be a silver bullet to solve every problem, it can provide an avenue to deal with challenges constructively.

TAKEAWAYS AND REFLECTIONS

PEOPLE SKILLS MATTER. It is important to develop self-awareness and awareness of others. Read the room and adjust your approach. Invite people in and ask for their perspectives.

THE CONCEPT OF EMOTIONAL INTELLIGENCE IS EVOLVING. Emotions are complex and we are continuing to learn about emotional intelligence. Still, it can be helpful to build self-awareness and empathy, and learn how to regulate your emotions.

EMOTIONS ARE PART OF THE HUMAN EXPERIENCE. Emotions are a normal part of the human experience, and there are no good or bad emotions. What you do with your emotions is important.

DO A ROOT CAUSE ANALYSIS. Investigate why you feel the way you do and refrain from judgment.

EXPAND YOUR SELF-AWARENESS. Learn more about yourself, including your triggers and typical responses. Notice how your emotions show up in your body so you can recognize when you are triggered. Examine how you feel and if your emotions are helping you or holding you back.

HAVE A FEW STRATEGIES TO REGULATE YOUR EMOTIONS. Experiment with a few coping strategies and see what works in different situations. Consider how you can cultivate better habits or employ strategies to modulate your emotions.

EXPAND YOUR SOCIAL AND CULTURAL HUMILITY. How we express, value, and regulate emotions varies across different cultures. Cultivate cultural humility and learn about people at the individual level.

EMOTIONAL INTELLIGENCE CAN HELP WITH EMOTIONAL LABOR. Emotional labor means managing your emotions for the requirements of the job. After doing that for an extended period of time, you might feel exhausted. Take breaks and have genuine conversations with people you trust.

3

WHAT COMES NEXT?

CHAPTER 10

BELIEVE IN BELONGING

Building community through belonging is important. However, belonging should never require abandoning your values and sense of self. When you learn to accept and embrace who you are, you will care less about external validation. You will show up with more confidence and ease and learn to appreciate self-belonging.

A digital agile leader can find and create belonging in different spaces. Let me illustrate with a story from my life.

My parents immigrated to the US in the early 1980s and we lived in a predominantly white neighborhood. At a young age, I knew I was different and grappled with my identity. Teachers would struggle as they landed upon my name during roll call.

However, as they moved effortlessly down the list to other classmates with names like Geoffrey, Mikaela, and Sebastian, I wondered, were these names any easier? Maybe not, but they were *familiar*.

As much as I thought blending in would make life easier, a part of me did not *want* to fit in and be like everyone else. I wanted to be me, but in a world that would embrace me. Yet, waiting on the world can be an exercise in futility.

Wherever I went, I had to learn to accept myself. Sometimes, I felt like I was not "Indian enough" around other Indians. In other spaces, I felt like an outsider when people would ask me, "Where exactly are *you* from?"

I grew accustomed to feeling nonbelonging. It was not until years later that I realized how not fitting in helped me to stand out—in a good way.

My mom played a significant role in my journey to self-acceptance. She was not always accepted, even within her community. Over time, she learned to embrace herself and march to the beat of her own drum. She continually inspires me to speak from the heart and celebrate who I am.

Your experiences might be different. What does belonging mean to you? Think about how you have assimilated to belong in a space, only to never truly belong. It can be exhausting trying to prove yourself to others and chase belonging at the expense of your identity and dignity.

People might not see you and all your gifts, despite your best efforts. The question is—how do you see yourself?

FIND BELONGING WITH DIFFERENT PEOPLE

You can find belonging in multiple and unexpected places. When I branched outside my comfort zone and connected with new people, I learned that I could create belonging intentionally.

I first met Jiya, an exchange student from Taiwan, when we were roommates in college. We communicated through eye contact and food more than words. I paid attention to the slight changes in her body language as she animatedly shared details of her day.

Sometimes we would eat together in comfortable silence.

One afternoon, she retrieved a book from her room and showed me photographs of her friends and family. Through these photos, I learned much about her. I could sense the same kind and cheerful energy in her pictures.

We were putting in the effort to learn about each other and create mutual belonging in our shared space.

How can you find and create belonging with others?

WHAT BELONGING FEELS LIKE

If you have ever felt out of place, you are not alone. When you start a new job or move to a new area, it might feel awkward at first as you find your footing in a new environment. Naturally, you might wonder if you will be accepted.

To gauge belonging, you might ask questions like:

- Do people know me? Do I know them?

- Do I try to connect with others? Are my efforts reciprocated?

- Can I be myself here?

- Am I treated with respect?

- Are my differences embraced?

- Do people ask me what I think?

- Do they listen?

- Do they care?

- Do I even *want* to be here?

Several factors contribute to feeling nonbelonging. If your skills are not being utilized or the role is different than you expected, you can feel out of place. If you are overlooked or excluded, that can feel demoralizing. Social anxiety and depression can also contribute to feelings of nonbelonging and vice versa.

Sometimes belonging feels challenging if we lack confidence in ourselves. Coaching can be helpful to build confidence and interpersonal skills.

Onboarding and training can also impact belonging. New employees may feel the training is not structured or sufficient enough to be successful in their role. While employees can benefit from learning how to adapt and be resourceful, leaders can also evaluate and improve processes.

As a digital agile leader, review your onboarding and training programs so employees can build connections and belonging from day one. Solicit input from people who are trying to speak up but struggling to be heard. Remind them that their ideas matter.

After discussing with hundreds of people and reflecting on my experiences, I gained insights into when belonging happens.

I feel like I belong when:
- I am invited *and* included.
- I can share my opinion, and when I do, I feel heard.
- I am respected.
- I feel safe.
- My uniqueness is accepted and celebrated.

I feel like I do not belong when:

- I am not included even though I am a key contributor.

- My opinion is not valued nor solicited.

- The conversation revolves around a topic that I do not know much about, or it is hard to get a word in edgewise.

- I lack sufficient training or resources to do my job.

- I feel the need to cover up my differences instead of being me.

- People assume I am like others with a similar background when I am not.

- I feel overlooked and underutilized.

Ask your employees how they define belonging, how important it is to them, and what they value.

"I feel like I belong when my ideas and opinions are welcome and encouraged," said Derek, an HR analyst.

"I was invited to the conversation, so I guess they were trying to include me," said Tamika, a senior manager at a financial services company. "But I didn't feel like I belonged. Everyone else received significantly more resources than me."

"Agree," said Anu, her colleague. "An invitation is not enough."

It took months before Gia felt like she belonged to her team. She had joined a company virtually and initially felt alone. "I had to make an effort to get to know people and build credibility," she shared. "After a few small wins and a team gathering, I finally felt like I belonged. Now I don't even give it a second thought."

Belonging can mean different things to different people. When do your employees feel out of place? If they do not feel like they belong, they may not stay long.

Sometimes you might overlook or forget to include people, not intentionally, but because you are trying to balance inclusivity with agility. You might need specific expertise and do not have time for multiple inputs and consensus. But belonging is not about including everyone in everything at every time.

You can foster belonging by modeling respect, showing appreciation, and listening. Speak up when you see exclusionary behavior and lead by example to enhance belonging.

OUT OF PLACE

Over the years, I have met many people who felt out of place for various reasons and they usually had one foot out the door. They may have:

- Outgrown their environment
- Felt uncomfortable and unsure how to express themselves
- Misinterpreted someone's actions as excluding
- Been outright excluded

They said, *I feel like I belong when my managers*:

- Ask questions and make a genuine effort to get to know me, not just my work.

- Recognize when these questions feel intrusive, and I simply do not want to share.

- Provide actionable feedback and support my growth.

- Check in on me as needed, but also give me the freedom to execute the work.

- Trust me when I show I am capable.

- Share the credit.

- Create a supportive environment where I am valued.

- Understand we are all human. I have my off days, just like they do, and we can learn from them.

Can you detect when your employees have one foot out the door and well before two feet?

In an increasingly complex world, it remains important to check in with your employees. This, of course, is different from being a "helicopter" manager and intervening in every decision. Some employees may need more frequent check-ins, while others are more self-directed. In remote and dispersed teams, fostering belonging can be challenging. It requires intentional outreach, coming together, and building community.

THE DIGITAL AGILE LEADER

BELONGING TAKES EFFORT

Belonging might feel easier in some spaces. Can you think of a space where you seamlessly belong?

Maybe you met someone and instantly clicked as if you were resonating at the same frequency. Or you reunited with a group of friends and picked up where you left off, regardless of how long it had been since you connected. You do not have to think about belonging; it happens naturally.

Even so, belonging can still require mutual effort and reciprocity. Is it realistic to feel a sense of belonging all the time? Will there be moments you feel left out or excluded, either intentionally or not? People can be nice and try to make you feel welcome, and you can *still* feel like you do not belong to a group or share the same values.

BELONG TO YOURSELF

Not belonging is not always bad; it could signal you are meant to be somewhere else. Recognize when you do not *want* to be somewhere so you can move on and not force-fit belonging.

Be mindful when you compromise parts of your identity to belong. If you are dimming your light and shrinking to fit in with a group, you might lose yourself in the name of belonging.

For me, wanting to belong meant I would always *be longing* to be accepted and understood. The feeling of belonging had to originate within myself first and foremost. When I learned to accept and embrace who I was, I cared less about external validation. I showed up with more confidence and ease in different situations, and I learned to appreciate solitude and self-belonging.

Here are some lessons I learned that might be helpful for you:

- Create inclusive spaces and speak up if you see exclusionary behavior.

- Foster belonging by branching out of your comfort zone and connecting with different people.

- Do not immediately cave in to the thought that you do not belong somewhere. Belonging does not always happen immediately.

- Make an effort to belong by actively participating and building connections.

- Reframe what belonging means. You belong when you can stay true to yourself.

- Practice self-acceptance, so whether or not you feel you belong in a group, you still belong to yourself.

- If you do not feel valued where you are, ask specifically for what you need. Or find and build community elsewhere.

- Find unconditional belonging with family and friends.

- Even when you walk alone, you are never alone.

TAKEAWAYS AND REFLECTIONS

BELONGING IS INTENTIONAL. In dispersed teams, fostering belonging can be challenging. It requires intentional outreach and community building. Maximize days in the office with purposeful agendas that include team building, collaborating, and learning.

BUILD BELONGING FROM THE BEGINNING. Starting from day one, welcome new employees and facilitate connections. Consider offering mentorship opportunities, training, business resource groups, team building, and check-ins to encourage a sense of belonging.

BELONGING IS PERSONAL. Ask your employees what belonging means to them.

BELONGING MAY NOT HAPPEN ALL THE TIME AND IN ALL SPACES. When you do not feel like you belong anywhere, reconnect to yourself and your truth. Examine your lens and reframe what belonging means. Do you automatically assume you do not belong somewhere based on your past experiences? What if you took ownership of belonging rather than waiting for others to give you permission? Know the value you bring simply because of who you are.

BELONG TO YOURSELF. Be mindful when you compromise your values or identity to belong somewhere. What are you giving up in the name of belonging? When you stay true to yourself, you might not belong somewhere, and that is okay.

BELONG TO A COMMUNITY. If you are not sure where you belong, reach out to others, return to your roots, and find a community that supports you. Go out there and find your place in the world. You may be holding yourself back from meeting people and forming new friendships, which can contribute to loneliness. Expand beyond your immediate social network and interact with different people.

CHAPTER 11

PLAY THE LONG GAME

Company politics is my least favorite "game" and sometimes the best move is to walk away. You might be lucky enough to watch politics from the sidelines. Or you could be shielded from politics altogether. Whatever your situation, be aware of your role and whether you want to engage.

In many cases, you will need to learn how to navigate politics. Avoiding politics is not always possible and could prevent you from growing and learning valuable leadership lessons. This does not mean you need to become hyperpolitical or compromise your values.

You may have seen leaders take politics to extremes and become greedy and reckless when faced with the lure of fame, money, or power. These leaders fall into the ego trap and play the short game. The short game is rooted in fear and driven by personal agendas. People who play the short game are trying desperately to compete and survive. But work doesn't have to be a zero-sum game.

THE EGO TRAP

The ego helps us survive and move through difficult situations with confidence. When left unchecked, however, the ego can become the Achilles' heel and culminate in a leader's downfall. It can also result in the downfall of an entire group, institution, or society and, in extreme cases, lead to violence and suffering. That does not mean we need to eradicate the ego; it means we learn how to manage it, so it does not manage us.

The eminent psychologist Carl Jung proposed that we all have a "shadow self" that comprises our blind spots and aspects of our personality we suppress—like impulses, doubts, and fears.[45] It is better to accept and understand our shadows, rather than deny and avoid them.

Shadow work is the process of making the unconscious conscious so you can acknowledge hidden parts of yourself. Journaling, reflecting, and therapy are some ways to do this. Shadow work is not about becoming perfect; it is about facing all sides of yourself, as uncomfortable as that may be.

Sometimes the shadows run much darker. Researchers Delroy L. Paulhus and Kevin M. Williams coined the term *The Dark Triad* in 2002. It refers to a trio of negative personality traits—narcissism, Machiavellianism, and psychopathy.[46] This can show up as grandiosity, unethical decision-making, exploitation, deception, and lack of remorse. These negative traits can disturb the social fabric of a group and ultimately hurt performance via retaliatory behaviors that cascade throughout the organization.[47]

Digital agile leaders work on their shadows and tame their egos in favor of the broader team and collective good. They play the long game.

WHAT IS THE LONG GAME?

The long game includes your:

- Relationships
- Integrity
- Character
- Well-being

Playing the long game means acting with integrity. It means to learn from your mistakes and pick and choose your battles. It means to understand the bigger picture and the importance of well-being. It also entails being a valuable partner and building authentic relationships.

BE A VALUABLE PARTNER

How much time do you spend building cross-functional relationships? It is convenient, especially in remote environments, to stay close to your immediate team. Without building broader relationships, you can inadvertently foster physical and learning silos.

Microsoft found that collaboration diminished with remote work when people stayed close to their project teams and spent less time building connections elsewhere. This created cracks in informal collaboration.[48]

Be mindful if you are siloing yourself within your team instead of connecting to different people. To be a digital agile leader, it is important to have a partnership mindset and develop relationships across the organization.

I have seen it firsthand: partnerships built in good faith can help you overcome obstacles that have been cemented in place for years. By contrast, individualistic goals, turf wars, and infighting can create wedges between groups and limit progress.

Relationships are important catalysts for progress. This does not mean relying solely on relationships to get things done. You also need to hold people accountable and understand the work.

DEMONSTRATE PARTNERSHIP ACTIONS

Whatever your role is in the organization—how can you be a better partner? What are some realistic goals you can set? Perhaps you can schedule a quick chat with someone and spend a few minutes learning about their scope of work. Or you can define ways to collaborate and lean on each other to deliver value.

As I walked the floors of a manufacturing company, I learned much from my colleagues. I observed how a shipping delay could lead to a product substitution. I learned how a new process could improve speed to market. I understood how the operations and support teams collaborated to rebuild customer loyalty. I would seek out knowledge and try to integrate it into my work. This seek-and-learn practice helped me understand the interconnected efforts of everyone.

I became a trusted advisor, and people shared information with me that empowered better decision-making.

If the culture is reserved, it can be hard to gather insights. You can still be a partner by showing support and actively collaborating with others. Assume good intent, make an effort, and express gratitude. Expressing gratitude has been shown to improve relationships and stress responses in teams.[49]

When you focus only on your work, you may not fully appreciate the contributions from other teams. As one technology leader implored, "Stakeholders across the business need to take a vested interest in how technology comes together. They expect the IT team to deliver quickly. But they are not thinking about the impact on our team and how technology works. Then when things go wrong, guess who is to blame? We are."

Another project leader, Uma, remarked, "My team has worked incredibly hard on revamping processes and strategy. It would be nice if our partners across the business could acknowledge and appreciate how hard we've worked and not just point out issues. We could use better partnership from our colleagues."

CONNECT THE CHASM

Often, I am engaged to improve collaboration and resolve chasms between teams. These chasms can exist for various reasons. New employees may come in and disrupt tenured employees who are used to specific ways of working. People might feel demotivated from a lack of trust, so they build walls to protect themselves and conserve energy. As a result, collaboration is short-lived and superficial.

Repairing chasms is not a quick fix, but it is possible. Sometimes, the issues are systemic and call for bigger changes. This requires leadership commitment, flexibility, and partnership across different groups.

INVEST IN WELL-BEING

Work can be rewarding and fulfill a sense of purpose. But taking care of your health can reap even bigger rewards. When it comes to the long game, well-being is a key component. This includes your physical, financial, social, emotional, spiritual, and mental well-being—which are intertwined. On a scale of one to ten, with ten being the highest, how would you rate your well-being in these different areas?

When was the last time you checked in with yourself and your employees? No one is immune to distress and illness. One in five US adults have a mental illness in any given year.[50] American actor Glenn Close said, "What mental health needs is more sunlight, more candor, and more unashamed conversation."

As she reflected on her prominent role in *Fatal Attraction*, she regretted playing into the stereotypes of mental illness. "When someone is being perceived as mentally unbalanced, it's very easy to make them the antagonist."[51]

By removing shame from the conversation, you can bring light to different topics. Why should we care about employee mental health? For a few reasons:

- Poor mental health and stress can negatively affect job performance, productivity, and communication.[52] Depression is estimated to cause 200 million lost workdays each year at a cost to employers of $17–$44 billion.[53]

- People experiencing mental health symptoms report they are unproductive for about 3.25 hours during the typical workday.[54]

Keep in mind the culture at work could be a source of distress. How is the culture reinforcing illness or wellness?

PREVENT BURNOUT

The world of work is evolving, and we are prone to more stress and burnout as we try to keep pace. Seventy percent of people experienced burnout in the last year across seven countries.[55] In 2019, The World Health Organization officially added *burnout* to the International Classification of Diseases.[56]

Burnout arises from chronic stress that has not been successfully managed. Because different factors can contribute to burnout, it is important to ask why and investigate the root cause.

Leaders today are expected to be coaches, visionaries, and strategists. Adding therapist to the list of demands can feel insurmountable. But you do not have to have all the answers or solve all the problems. If you are not qualified or able to provide support, find out what resources are available.

BUILD PSYCHOLOGICAL SAFETY

To complicate matters, employees may not want to disclose their struggles, especially in the workplace, where it may not feel safe to share. Employees understandably could be concerned with how they might be perceived and if they will lose their job.

Over the years, people have told me why they do not feel comfortable sharing. They said:

- In the past when I shared, I received a negative response from others. I have learned it is not okay to share.

- I think other people have it worse than me, so I am not allowed to feel a certain way because I do not have it "that bad."

- I do not want to be perceived as less competent.

- It is hard to say what I want to say. I feel like communication is difficult for me, probably stemming from a lack of confidence.

- I need to watch what I say, so I do not say the wrong thing or in the wrong way. Especially since English is not my first language.

- I am afraid of saying the wrong thing and being misunderstood.

- What if my truth makes people think I am not qualified for my role? How might they perceive me?

- The more visible I become, the scarier it is to share. When I work behind the scenes, it's easier to drop the façade because there is less pressure.

- I simply do not want to share.

Dr. Amy Edmondson, Harvard Business School professor, introduced the term *psychological safety* as a belief that one will not be punished or humiliated for speaking up with ideas, questions, concerns, or mistakes.[57]

Lack of psychological safety could result in employees becoming quiet, accepting the status quo, and competing instead of collaborating. Digital agile leaders can build psychological safety by being open to feedback, building trust, and providing multiple ways to share information. They can also normalize and discuss how sharing can be difficult for anyone.

It takes courage to share out loud. It also takes courage to create a space where it is not only possible to share—it is safe. And where it is also safe to *not* share.

ASK HOW ARE YOU?

As a leader, you will encounter different challenges. You do not have to jump in and try to fix every issue; instead, hold the space and listen. Start by asking, *How can I support you? What's on your mind?* or simply, *How are you?*

When you ask someone, "How are you?" the typical response is "fine" or "good." Yet 84 percent of employees reported that they rarely mean it every time they say they are "fine" or "good."[58]

When you ask, "How are you?" allow that question to linger for a few seconds and read the room. Do not take it personally if your employees do not want to share their thoughts. Simply respect their position and remind them you are there if needed. By being present and showing support, you can connect on a genuine level.

STAY CONNECTED

There is significant evidence that feeling connected can improve our immune system, longevity, and mental well-being.[59] Humans are wired to connect, and this connection affects our health.

Yet 58 percent of US adults feel lonely. Studies have shown that loneliness and poor social connections are as bad for your health as smoking fifteen cigarettes a day.[60] Some people are impacted more than others, including people from underrepresented groups.[61]

Technology has been instrumental in breaking down boundaries and seamlessly connecting people across geographies. However, excessive technology usage can contribute to isolation and loneliness. While technology has expanded how we connect, facilitating *intentional* connection is up to each of us.

How can you connect more intentionally? Are you trying to connect but not going much deeper than surface-level interactions? Reinforce connections by showing genuine interest and talking about shared and individual goals.

LIGHTEN THE LOAD

Another way to connect is through kindness and humor. Despite the challenges, work does not have to be serious all the time. When the energy feels heavy and emotions are supercharged, lighten the load.

I have had many moments of laughter and fun at work and use humor as a healing force. Humor is crucial. You are meant to laugh, feel joy, and have fun, not just struggle and endure pain.

Having fun can sometimes feel like a luxury when there is chaos and uncertainty. But fun can be restorative and remind you that there is more to your lived experience.

Where can you inject humor and fun to heal your relationships and add levity to otherwise heavy spaces (where appropriate)? The purpose of humor is not to minimize important and difficult conversations but to connect with others through our humanity.

LISTEN TO DATA AND INTUITION

Take a moment to reconnect with yourself. What do you really need? As a leader, you may want to keep a mask on and show strength all the time. The truth is no one is invincible.

"Believe me, I feel the intensity of everything that's going on right now," admitted Petra, a VP of marketing.

She paused and looked at the weary audience. Petra felt distance between them, and she wanted to close the gap. It was becoming harder to maintain a veneer of strength.

"These are challenging times, and I may never fully understand how some of you feel," she continued. "While I don't have the answers, I recognize we all need to do better and give each other grace."

Petra relied on data and her intuition as she navigated the conversation.

We all have intuition, or inner wisdom. While not infallible, your intuition can help you under stress or in complex decision-making. Studies suggest that intuition is a highly complex and developed form of reasoning based on experience, learning, patterns, and abstractions stored in your head.[62]

Sometimes the best voice to listen to is the one within you. Well-meaning people can give you good advice, but you may intuitively know the best course of action. Your intuition serves a purpose and can be a helpful guide on your journey. You can develop your intuition by meditating, journaling, asking questions, and testing your intuitive responses.

If we rely only on intuition, we may ignore important data. Using widely available data, however, does not always lead to effective decisions. And bad data can lead to false confidence. Critical thinking and reasoning are therefore important when making decisions. Try to balance intuition with data and apply a hybrid approach to decision-making.

As a leader, you may have limited time to make complex decisions. Decision fatigue can set in when you feel tired or overwhelmed. Consider how you can simplify decision-making. If you can standardize processes or ask for help, you can free up your mental energy to make bigger decisions.

MAKE A DECISION

How do you make decisions? Let's say you are planning a vacation. Do you spend hours researching flights and planning your itinerary? Do you want to please everyone? Do you feel anxiety making a decision? Do people tell you, "You are indecisive" or "Just make a decision"?

You are not alone. Being analytical is a strength. But you might get stuck in analysis paralysis and planning mode. How can you switch from planning to execution?

Colin Powell, former US Secretary of State, created the 40/70 rule that states you need between 40 and 70 percent of the total information to make a decision. With less than 40 percent, you can make a poor choice, and with more than 70 percent, you will wait too long and become overwhelmed.

Another decision-making tool is the OODA loop developed by military strategist and United States Air Force Colonel John Boyd. OODA stands for Observe, Orient, Decide, and Act. This process favors agility since you observe and react to events as they happen. OODA is a continuous feedback loop of observing, analyzing data, making a decision, and monitoring the decision. With continuous feedback, you adjust and learn, and the next loop becomes faster and more accurate.

When making decisions, weigh the pros and cons, consult with others, and evaluate the risks and alternatives. Do the best you can with what you have and remain agile.

PLAY THE LONG GAME

The game of work can be tumultuous. As you honor your commitments to others, think about the commitments you have made to yourself. Take care of yourself so you have the longevity to lead. Find joy in fleeting moments of connection, and embrace all that is human, not just the serious sides.

Make time for rest and replenishment so you can last as a leader. Remember what you are grateful for and the importance of connections. Build a supportive environment where people feel safe, valued, and respected.

Play the long game.

TAKEAWAYS AND REFLECTIONS

BUILD RELATIONSHIPS. Actively develop cross-functional relationships. Learn about areas outside your domain, develop a partnership mindset, and back it up with actions.

TAME YOUR EGO. We all have egos. The ego can help us push through fear with confidence. But egos can also cause irreparable damage if left unchecked.

INTEGRATE WELL-BEING. Well-being encompasses your physical, mental, social, emotional, financial, and spiritual state. Evaluate how to integrate work with well-being, and seek support when stress persists. While we may be able to rely on others, we need to be responsible for our own well-being.

BUILD PSYCHOLOGICAL SAFETY. Create a place where people feel safe expressing their concerns and talking about mistakes. In places that lack psychological safety, employees may withhold information and mistakes can go unnoticed until it is too late.

REVIEW AND REBALANCE. Leadership is about optimizing team efforts and making difficult decisions. Give yourself credit for what you are doing well. Extend and share credit with the team.

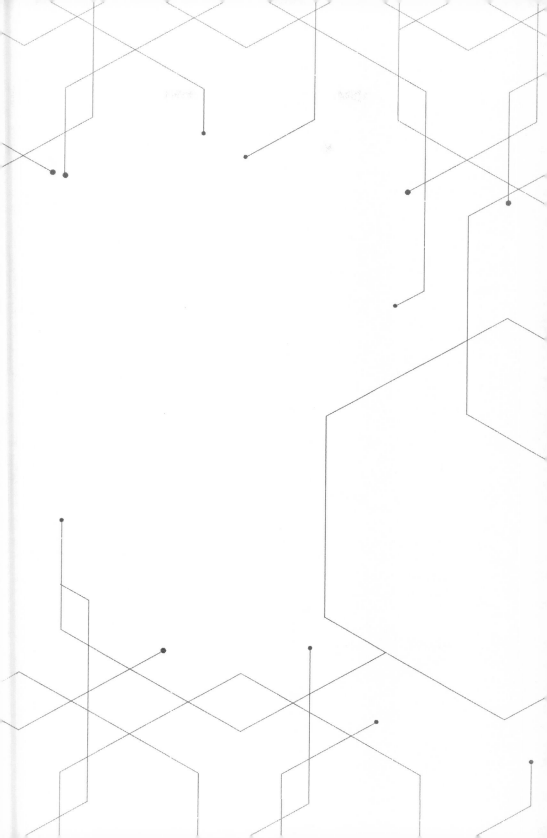

CHAPTER 12

THE FUTURE OF LEADING
IN A DIGITAL AGE

A marketing manager at a technology company—let's call her Rita—took off her shoe and hurled it against the wall. Everyone stared in shock as Rita cursed expletives at her computer.

"Why do we need to *change*?" she screamed in frustration.

"Rita, I understand this is frustrating," I said. "Let's take a minute."

She stepped outside and pulled her cashmere shawl tightly around her arms. The windchill grew intense, and the sky turned a deep gray. Rita admitted she was mostly frustrated with herself. The company was implementing new processes and she felt very uncomfortable.

"Things are changing so fast. It's hard to learn all this new stuff," she admitted.

"You're absolutely right, Rita," I said. "Change is difficult. But you can learn this. With practice and effort, it will get easier. And we are here to support you."

Over the next few weeks, I met with Rita to understand her pain points and knowledge gaps. By the end of the project, she became one of our biggest champions. She even trained and onboarded new hires to the platform.

LISTEN TO THE PUSHBACK

Change can be frustrating. In Rita's case, she realized she was mostly frustrated with herself. She did not want to feel incompetent in her role as she learned new ways of working.

When frustrations naturally arise, take a moment to reflect. What are you frustrated with specifically? Think about the last time you learned something new. It might have felt frustrating to start over and shift your existing mental models.

You may be familiar with the quote, "Be the change you wish to see." I also like to say be *in* the change. Show the team that you are willing to roll up your sleeves and do the work. At the same time, listen to the pushback. Resistance is not all bad. People may have valid reasons for resisting change. What are they (or you) resisting and why?

DIGITAL AGILE LEADER LESSON

Be in the change.

Think about something that changed in your life to the extent that you cannot imagine going back. Maybe it is how you shop, communicate, or listen to music. Reflect on how you navigated change, what you learned, and how you can move through this next wave of change.

When I think of a change in my lifetime, music comes to mind. As a teenager, I visited my local music shop and browsed through cassettes and CDs. Today, we can access music through the cloud, live stream concerts, and participate in immersive virtual experiences. We can sort, store, and share music in the blink of an eye. Yet, a classic vinyl record still holds value. As for the music itself, well, we all have our opinions.

What was different for you five or ten years ago? How did you adjust? What makes change hard for you now? Sometimes change is hard because you want to honor and preserve something special about the past. You might want to feel more prepared and optimistic before you embark on a new path.

FIND OPTIMISM

It is hard to remain optimistic about the future, especially when things are changing so fast. If you can find *something* to be grateful for, it can help you persevere through tough times. When you persevere, you can still encounter obstacles, but you learn from them and forge onward. Build resilience by seeking support, reflecting on past successes, and challenging limiting beliefs.

During transitions, there may be obstacles and suffering, yet you should never underestimate the strength of the human spirit and the power within you.

DIGITAL AGILE LEADER LESSON

Never underestimate the strength of the human spirit and the power within you.

If you feel overwhelmed or stuck, ask yourself:

· What can I control?

· What is one thing I can do now?

· What does a contingency plan look like?

· What else is possible?

· What do I need?

· Where can I go for support?

· How can I be a source of support for someone else?

DIGITAL AGILE LEADER LESSON

When all hope seems lost, find some anyway.

THE FUTURE OF LEADING IN A DIGITAL AGE

Optimism and preparation are key as we encounter more change. The graph that follows shows that as the pace of innovation increases, the waves of time are compressed.[63] The next waves could be even

shorter in duration. Advancements in AI, robotics, and other disruptive technologies could affect how we live and work. It remains
to be seen how far some of these innovations will go and what is
next on the horizon.

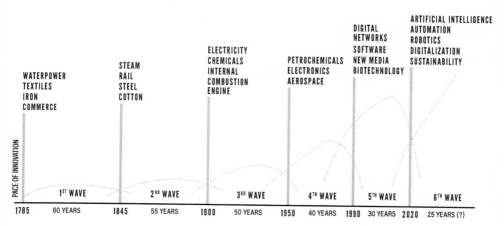

In an ever-changing digital world, it is important to remain
curious and discerning. Consider the impact of innovation by
reflecting on these questions:

- What are the costs and benefits of the innovation?
- Where are skills gaps, and how can you bridge them?
- What questions do you need to ask? What answers do you
  need to question?

Innovation will bring about shifts in how we live and work. It could
alter the types of jobs and expand project- and skills-based work. It
could shift the leader-team dynamic and favor a more bottom-up
leadership approach where people closest to the work can make

decisions. We could see expansion in the gig economy as people select projects and create a career model that works for them.

Some jobs will be eliminated while new ones are created, as we have seen before. Yet, humans will still be vital to the workplace for the foreseeable future.

In their publication *Socially Responsible Automation: A Framework For Shaping The Future*, Pramod Khargonekar and Meera Sampath suggest:[64]

1. Humans will and should remain critical and central to the workplace of the future.

2. Automation, artificial intelligence, and related technologies are but tools to improve and enrich human lives and livelihoods.

How is your industry and workplace evolving? What competencies will you need in the next three to five years? How can you plan for these changes? You may not have all the answers, but you can stay informed and reevaluate your priorities at different crossroads.

THE DIGITAL PARADOX

While we have reaped many benefits from innovation, we may simultaneously be concerned about the long-term effects. We may want technology to automate mundane and dangerous tasks, but we are also concerned about the impact of ongoing advancement. We do not want to overautomate and lose the human touch.

Therein lies the digital paradox.

How can we innovate without unintended consequences? There are no perfect solutions. We need to be *digitally wise* and consider the impact of technology on people and the planet. This requires radical collaboration and a holistic view that considers ethical, legal, societal, and economic implications.

As Henry A. Kissinger, Eric Schmidt, and Daniel Huttenlocher aptly state in their book, *The Age of AI: And Our Human Future*, "While the advancement of AI may be inevitable, its ultimate destination is not."[65]

I agree that shaping our destination (and destiny) needs to be a collective effort and an integrative approach that combines different perspectives. Remember to remain hopeful about the future, no matter what fears may shroud your view.

DIGITAL AGILE LEADER LESSON

Not all change is bad;
opportunities exist in endings and beginnings.

KNOW YOUR WHAT, WHY, HOW, AND WHO

Regardless of the change you are making, know your *what, why, how,* and *who*. What are you changing, how are you changing it, and why? Who does it impact? After all, it is not just about implementing change; it is also about doing it thoughtfully.

Change for the sake of change can be costly. I have seen companies embark on expensive transformation projects and scale back once they realize they are only benefitting from a thin slice. I have seen leaders throw change like spaghetti on the wall to see what sticks without considering the impact on the people.

I have seen the opposite too, where large corporations move so slowly that they fall behind their competitors and get trapped in analysis paralysis. Or they roll out a solution and stick with it for decades, even though it slows down the business.

Every organization is different. Try to understand the history, industry, culture, feasibility, and appetite for change. Before propelling toward change, take a step back and review change in the context of your situation. Why are you making a change? What future state do you envision? What is not working in the current state?

THE FUTURE IS FLEXIBLE

The future can take on different forms. I regularly speak at conferences on various topics, including change and technology. In many ways, emerging technologies are still evolving, and it will be interesting to see how things play out over the next decade. As trends collide, some things will stick, some will fall off the hype curve, and some will take years to reach mainstream adoption.

You might be thinking, *That's nice, but we are so far behind in our digital journey that all this new stuff seems farfetched.* And you might be right. Perhaps you are trying to modernize your core infrastructure to enable innovation and secure the future.

Consider the next feasible step in your digital journey. Learn what it takes to implement and maintain the technology. What are the pros and cons? What are the costs? What are more cost-effective options? How will you support the new technology after it has been implemented?

You do not have to become a technology enthusiast, but you can stay curious so you do not fall behind the curve. How can you be a more *digitally curious* leader? How can you innovate *with purpose*?

It is important to understand the impact of innovation and not just chase headlines and media impressions. At the same time, be open to what the future can bring and be willing to experiment. Futures thinking can be a helpful exercise to explore the possibilities.

FUTURES THINKING AND CREATIVITY

Futures thinking helps you identify emerging trends and predict different scenarios. While predictions can be wrong, and the future is uncertain, you can still imagine *potential* futures.

Imagine it is ten years from now. What does the world look like? We might be more immersed in digital devices. Or perhaps we spend more time in nature and reduce our dependence on technology.

You can future-think the possibilities for your life or career and set specific goals. What are some projects you want to tackle or markets you want to enter? Who do you want to be? What aspects of your life do you want to change?

When you imagine future possibilities, you connect with your creative side. Ursula Le Guin, an American author, said, "The creative adult is the child who survived." As a child, perhaps you approached life with a sense of reckless abandon, wonder, and play. Over the years, you may have lost confidence in yourself and your creative abilities.

We are all creative in our own ways. If you solve problems, build things, or have a unique point of view—that is creative. If you find your way through obstacles or connect abstract thoughts—that is creative. Creativity is about generating ideas and looking at problems in new ways. Think about how you are already engaging in creative expression in your life.

GO WITH THE FLOW

During the creative process, you might enter into a state of flow. Flow is a cognitive state when you are completely immersed in an activity. It involves focus, engagement, and the loss of awareness of time and self.

The concept of flow was coined by Hungarian American psychologist Mihaly Csikszentmihalyi. In the 1960s, he studied the creative process and found that when an artist was in flow, they would persist at their task relentlessly. He also found that the artist would lose interest after the project was completed, highlighting the importance of the *process* and not the end result.[66]

It is normal to encounter creative blocks when you feel stuck. Perfectionistic tendencies and self-doubt can arise. Take a break, try again later, and remind yourself what you enjoy about the process. Schedule some fun in your calendar to reignite your creative spark.

You can tap into your creativity in many ways, including seeking multiple answers, doodling (which I do often), stepping into nature, or even with a practice known as mind wandering. It has been shown that the human mind wanders 30 to 50 percent of waking time.[67] When you allow your mind to wander, you can explore new ideas and imagine possibilities.

When your mind wanders, follow it and see where it goes. What do you envision for the future?

PRACTICE CREATIVITY AND FUTURES THINKING

Below is an exercise I developed to foster futures thinking and creativity.

Example 1: Describe something from the past. Does it still exist, or has it changed? How is it different today? What might it look like in the future?

Example 2: Write down something you accomplished in the past. What are you doing today? What might you want to do in the future?

WHAT WAS	WHAT IS	WHAT COULD BE
We needed separate devices to take photos, make phone calls, and browse the internet.	We can use a single device for multiple applications.	There will be additional integrations and interoperability across platforms and devices.
I was a student studying engineering.	I am developing a new product at work.	I want to start a business and have funding to scale my ideas.

The future never stops forming. The question is—will you fear it or face it? Will you be a part of the design or relinquish all power to others to determine your future?

The future cannot be self-centered; it needs to encompass teams, communities, and the world at-large. How can you collaborate with others to create the future?

Consider the following:

· **Be curious.** Ask, What if? What else? Why? Why not?

· **Prioritize.** What matters? Where should you focus your efforts and resources?

· **Seek and provide clarity.** Learn to become comfortable with some level of ambiguity. At the same time, seek and provide clarity along the way.

THE GIFT OF PRESENCE

Futures thinking can help you explore the possibilities. However, constantly thinking about the future (or past) can create unnecessary worry. If that happens, return to the present moment and focus on today.

Distractions may arise, but not all distractions are bad. Reconnect to the present moment through your breath and by engaging your senses. What sounds do you hear within and around you? What do you see, feel, taste, or smell?

Take a breath and ground yourself where you are. When you are grounded in the present, you can tune into your thoughts, pick up on cues, and find music between the notes. You can appreciate another person—their expressions, patterns, and pauses.

Set an intention to be more centered and present with others:

I am here with someone and that is a gift.

I am grateful for this moment.

I will find one thing to appreciate about where I am and who I am with.

This moment is here, and I am in it.

NOW IS HERE

Even as the present keeps shifting, you have the power to do something now. Start by looking at your situation. What is changing? How can you show up better for yourself and others?

Maybe you want to spend more time with family, pay off debt, volunteer, plan a trip, or grow your business. You could be on the cusp of making a courageous life decision that will take you down a new path. Your heart might be imploring you to have a conversation or repair a relationship with someone you love.

You might feel a sense of urgency to improve your situation, create a bigger impact in the world, or lead and live from the heart. What is one step forward you can take? What can you do today?

MY DIGITAL AGILE LEADERSHIP GUIDING PHRASES

In addition to the digital agile leader lessons I have shared throughout this book, I have also developed several guiding phrases to live by, including the following:

- I may fear change, but I remain curious about what it brings.
- I will notice something new today and appreciate its beauty.
- I will try to understand a problem before attempting to solve it.
- I appreciate the wisdom gained from failure.
- We are all connected, and our actions have ripple effects.
- The future is uncertain and the present is an opportunity to shape it.
- While I do not know exactly where my path might lead, I can try to pave it more intentionally.

What lessons have you learned along your path? What guiding phrases do you want to create for yourself? How can you be a digital agile leader?

TAKEAWAYS AND REFLECTIONS

BE DIGITALLY CURIOUS. You might shy away from technology or feel burdened by the cognitive load of learning something new. When technology seems daunting, curiosity can demystify it. Think about the use cases and application of technology. Honor your pace while keeping an open mind to learning something new.

TECHNOLOGY IS RAPIDLY ACCELERATING. You can ignore technology shifts or become curious about them. What is changing? How accessible and inclusive will the technology be? How can we bridge the growing digital divides?

LEARNING DOES NOT STOP. Whether it is the metaverse (or related technology), blockchain, web x.0, or another innovation, there will always be more change and The Next Iteration or The Next Big Thing. These technologies have the potential to disrupt industries and impact our lives. Many are still in the early stages and will require quantum leaps in computing and take years for adoption.

BE DISCERNING. It is okay to be skeptical and take a wait-and-see approach. Review different sources of information and be discerning.

DISRUPT YOUR MINDSET. Disruptive change requires disruptive thinking. Your fear should not just be of the new but of adhering to the old. How can you disrupt your status quo?

HELP YOURSELF AND OTHERS. Self-development is lifelong, continuous work. Only you will know when "being better" becomes good enough for you. In the quest for self-development, do not forget to extend support to others.

FINAL THOUGHTS

We can reminisce about the days of old with a sense of nostalgia. Yet, Pandora's box has flung open, and it is hard to go back to what was. There is no "normal"; there is only what we choose to normalize.

We will encounter change throughout our lives. Watching our loved ones (and ourselves) age is a stark reminder that nothing is permanent, that transitions are happening around us every day across generations.

In a world where things are constantly changing, one thing remains clear—we must remain adaptable.

For many of us, change is challenging, and we are all dealing with different things differently. Have compassion, grace, and patience for yourself and others. Think about where you might be getting comfortable and complacent in your life and how you can create small, albeit uncomfortable, shifts for growth. How can you lean into change?

Evaluate your situation and be honest when you are holding yourself (or others) back. Be mindful when internal or external voices keep you stuck. Remember the truth—you are powerful, change is inevitable, and the choice to adapt is yours.

The world is changing faster than we can keep up. There is no finish line, and things will keep shifting. Go at your own pace, as long as you go. Otherwise, you may be left behind.

DIGITAL AGILE LEADER LESSON

*Sometimes it takes a leap of faith
to leap forward into the unknown.*

ACKNOWLEDGMENTS

I would like to extend my heartfelt appreciation to my family—namely my parents, Gulshan and Rajni, and my siblings, Anjli, Pallavi, and Manoj.

The Moose in my Agility Matrix was inspired by a nickname given to me by my family and recently revived by my brother, Manoj. It is with deep gratitude and love that I weave this into my work.

To all my clients, colleagues, and friends who have supported me along the way—I appreciate you. Thank you for your support and partnership. They mean more than you know.

Over nine months, I spent countless hours writing and rewriting this book. I hope you find some inspiration or pieces of wisdom you can take with you.

Creating something new can be messy and frustrating, and at the same time, fun and rewarding. Throughout your journey, I encourage you to keep trying and believing in yourself. With time, you will see how your efforts matter and how bright your future can be.

ABOUT THE AUTHOR

Manisha Dhawan is an ICF-accredited coach, consultant, facilitator, speaker, and author with over two decades of experience working across multiple roles and industries. She started her career in her family business, Applied Membranes Inc., working with her father and mentor, Gulshan Dhawan, PhD.

Manisha also spent several years at organizations including PwC, Deloitte Consulting, Slalom, and Taco Bell Corp, leading global digital transformation and change management initiatives. She has led large-scale, complex technology implementations, successfully turned around stagnant projects, and built high-performing teams.

Through her company, MPath Coaching, Manisha develops more effective leaders and collaborative teams so organizations can attract and retain talent. Her services include executive and career coaching, organizational development consulting, customized workshops, trainings, and speaking engagements. Manisha's clients range from individuals to startups to Fortune 10 companies.

Manisha holds a BS in chemistry and an MBA from UC Irvine. She received her coaching certificate from iPEC. She has served as an adjunct professor at Cal State University San Marcos and a guest lecturer at UC Irvine. Manisha is certified in various assessments including CliftonStrengths, Emotional Intelligence, Everything DiSC, Energy Leadership Index, and Insights Discovery.

On a personal note, Manisha is passionate about building community and volunteering at various organizations. She enjoys spending time with family, traveling, and connecting with people. She currently resides in San Diego, California.

To contact Manisha, purchase copies of her book, or schedule her as a speaker, you may contact her at manisha@mpathcoaching.com or 714-468-5667.

ENDNOTES

1 According to the Gallup World Poll, the average full-time worker spends 41.36 hours per week working. If you assume people work 48 weeks per year, it means people spend 1,985.28 hours per year working. The current life expectancy is around 73 and retirement is about 63 years old. If people begin working at 22, then the average person works for 41 years. Forty-one years of work at 1,985.28 hours per year is 81,396 total hours. This estimate is conservative and may even be low. Another estimate finds that people work over 115,000 hours in a lifetime. Gallup State of the Global Workplace: 2022 Report.

2 Gallup finds 60 percent of people are emotionally detached at work and 19 percent are miserable. Gallup's technical term for being miserable at work is "actively disengaged." The terms for thriving at work and emotionally detached at work are "engaged" and "not engaged." Gallup State of the Global Workplace: 2022 Report.

3 Like alcohol, sleep deprivation also affects judgment, making it harder to assess how impaired you are when you are tired. https://healthysleep.med.harvard.edu/need-sleep/whats-in-it-for-you.

4 Code-switching involves adjusting one's style of speech, appearance, behavior, and expression in ways that will optimize the comfort of others in exchange for fair treatment, quality service, and employment opportunities." Courtney L. McCluney, et al., "The Costs Of Code-Switching," *Harvard Business Review*, 2019, https://hbr.org/2019/11/the-costs-of-codeswitching.

5   As a leading voice in the convergence of technology and health, John Nosta is regarded as a "top disruptor" in technology, innovation, life sciences, and the pharmaceutical industry. His article emphasizes how agility is not about speed. The instant gratification culture and the *I Want What I Want When I Want It* (IWWIWWIWI) mindset is not strategic nor agile. We may live in a culture of instant gratification, but that can be misleading because we may need to wait and go through the process. John Nosta, "Business, Don't Mistake Speed for Agility" *Psychology Today*, 2018, https://www.psychologytoday.com/us/blog/the-digital-self/201808/in-business-dont-mistake-speed-agility

6   In September 2022, Merriam-Webster added 370 new words to the dictionary across business, technology, food, and nature. New words include dumbphone (a smartphone without advanced features), metaverse, virtue signaling, and greenwash. Also included are slang words like janky (poor quality), sus (suspicious), and cringe (awkward). The dictionary chronicles how language grows and changes. This is true across multiple languages and dialects. https://www.merriam-webster.com/words-at-play/new-words-in-the-dictionary

7   Self-adjustment and receiving external support can help us adapt to new environments. This paper illustrates the importance of self-adjustment and social support for adaptability. The hypothesis is that social support will moderate the relationship between adaptability and life satisfaction. If adaptable individuals receive a high level of social support, it would be expected that they would be able to adapt well to the environment and have a high level of life satisfaction. By contrast, low levels of social support can decrease the level of life satisfaction. Mi Zhou and Weipeng Lin, "Adaptability And Life Satisfaction: The Moderating Role Of Social Support," 2016, https://www.ncbi.nlm.nih.gov/pmc/articles/PMC4963457/

8   In 2021 PwC conducted a Global Culture Survey of 3,200 leaders and employees worldwide. The data showed 67 percent of survey respondents said culture is more important than strategy or operations. They agreed that top cultural priorities should include recruitment and retention, digitization, health and safety, and collaboration. "Organizational Culture: It's Time To Take Action," 2021, https://www.pwc.com/gx/en/issues/upskilling/global-culture-survey-2021.html.

9   Daniel B. Griffith, "Debunking Misconceptions About Happiness At Work," 2022, https://www.higheredjobs.com/Articles/articleDisplay.cfm?ID=3152.

10   From my perspective, there may be a natural conflict between being vulnerable and being a leader, especially if you are in a high-visibility role. Leaders need to balance showing their emotions and containing them based on the audience and context, and recognize that while vulnerability has benefits, a leadership role may introduce other expectations. In her article, Minda Zetlin explores Brené Brown's work on the benefits of vulnerability. She counters this notion with a study conducted at the Georgia Institute of Technology that revealed vulnerability in the workplace can hurt you if you are in a leadership position. Minda Zetlin, "Showing Vulnerability At Work Can Hurt You If You're The Boss, Science Finds," 2019, https://www.inc.com/minda-zetlin/workplace-vulnerability-leaders-lose-authority.html.

11   James Ullrich, "Corporate Stockholm Syndrome: The US Workplace Suffers From A Rapidly Rising Problem," 2014, https://www.psychologytoday.com/us/blog/the-modern-time-crunch/201403/corporate-stockholm-syndrome.

12   We need to examine why we do things rather than blindly accepting the status quo, even for widely established constructs. For example,

lengthy goal-setting forms are outdated. The entire performance review process may benefit from a redesign, especially as the world of work changes. According to Gallup, only 14 percent of employees strongly agree that their performance reviews inspire them to improve. Robert Sutton and Ben Wigert, "More Harm Than Good: The Truth About Performance Reviews," 2019, https://www.gallup.com/workplace/249332/harm-good-truth-performance-reviews.aspx.

13 Kim Parker and Juliana Menasce Horowitz, "Majority Of Workers Who Quit A Job In 2021 Cite Low Pay, No Opportunities For Advancement, Feeling Disrespected," 2022, https://www.pewresearch.org/fact-tank/2022/03/09/majority-of-workers-who-quit-a-job-in-2021-cite-low-pay-no-opportunities-for-advancement-feeling-disrespected/.

14 There is debate as to when design thinking first originated. As design thinking has increased in popularity over the years, many people have jumped on the buzz train. The global design agency IDEO popularized design thinking and they have been using it since 1978 across multiple contexts. But design thinking encompasses more than a one-time workshop or brainstorming session. Embedding design thinking within an organization is challenging and not without its limitations. https://designthinking.ideo.com/faq/how-do-people-define-design-thinking.

15 The First Principles method explained by Elon Musk in an interview with Kevin Rose: https://www.youtube.com/watch?v=NV3sBlRgzTI.

16 Researchers have refuted his theory and proposed that "mastery" depends on the student's teacher and their ability to see the student individually. Opposing research also showed that some of the best performers practiced less, and that other factors like genetics, personality, and access to resources play an important role. We may not become experts at something no matter how much we practice, so we should not hold ourselves to impossible standards. Malcolm

Gladwell, *Outliers: The Story Of Success* (New York: Little, Brown and Company, 2008).

17   Whether you aspire to be "pretty good" or "great" at something, practice is important. Josh Kaufman suggests the first 20 hours of practice—or 45 minutes per month – can help you move from knowing nothing to being "pretty good." Practice can be difficult, especially when starting something new. We may lack confidence or resources, or minimize the importance of practicing a skill. However, practice can help us course correct and refine our approach. Josh Kaufman: The First 20 Hours: How to Learn Anything Fast (New York: Penguin Group, 2014).

18   "Study Shows How Taking Short Breaks May Help Our Brains Learn New Skills," *National Institute Of Neurological Disorders And Stroke* (NINDS), 2021, https://www.nih.gov/news-events/news-releases/study-shows-how-taking-short-breaks-may-help-our-brains-learn-new-skills.

19   WD-40 is one of many examples where a team's first product iteration "failed." But eventually the team developed a formula that worked. In fact, the product worked so well that several employees snuck cans of WD-40 Multi-Use Product out of the plant in their lunch-boxes to use at home. WD-40 Company, https://wd40company.com/our-company/our-history/.

20   David Kindy, "The Accidental Invention Of Bubble Wrap," 2019, https://www.smithsonianmag.com/innovation/accidental-invention-bubble-wrap-180971325/

21   "Cosmic Milestone: NASA Confirms 5,000 Exoplanets," NASA Jet Propulsion Laboratory, California Institute of Technology, 2022, https://www.jpl.nasa.gov/news/cosmic-milestone-nasa-confirms-5000-exoplanets

22 In his article, Maclen Stanley shares how purpose is correlated with health, wealth, and happiness. And people at every stage of life are happier when they possess a sense of purpose. Of course, the definition of happiness can vary. Maclen Stanley, "Three Crucial Discoveries About Purpose In Life," 2021, https://www.psychologytoday.com/us/blog/making-sense-chaos/202109/3-crucial-discoveries-about-purpose-in-life

23 PwC's Putting Purpose To Work Survey was based on 1,510 full and part-time employees and 502 business leaders in 39 industries around the US. "Putting Purpose To Work: A Study Of Purpose In The Workplace," PwC, 2016, https://www.pwc.com/us/en/about-us/corporate-responsibility/assets/pwc-putting-purpose-to-work-purpose-survey-report.pdf

24 Manfred Max-Neef's Fundamental Human Needs taxonomy was published for the first time in 1986. No consensus exists about the exact meaning of 'human need." Rodrigo Cardoso, Ali Sobhani, and Evert Meijers, "The Cities We Need: Towards An Urbanism Guided By Human Needs Satisfaction," 2021, https://journals.sagepub.com/doi/full/10.1177/00420980211045571#bibr37-00420980211045571

25 Cardozo et al., "The Cities We Need." 2021, https://journals.sagepub.com/doi/full/10.1177/00420980211045571#bibr37-00420980211045571

26 In this article, Enright suggests Maslow's hierarchy, especially the level of esteem, needs reconstruction. In countries where so many people's basic needs are met, there are considerably higher divorce rates, and the quest for esteem can lead to self-absorption and narcissism. Enright underscores how we can learn a lot from people who struggle with the basics of life and still rise to make a difference. Robert Enright, "Why Maslow's Self-Actualization Theory Is Not Quite Right: Having All Needs Met And Living With Little Suffering May Stifle Growth," 2018, https://www.psychologytoday.com/

us/blog/the-forgiving-life/201805/why-maslows-self-actualization-theory-is-not-quite-right

27 Ikigai is a Japanese concept referring to something that gives a person a sense of purpose, or a reason for living. It combines the terms iki, meaning "alive" or "life," and gai, meaning "benefit" or "worth." When combined, these terms mean that which gives your life worth, meaning, or purpose. Ikigai also appears related to the concept of flow, as described in the work of Hungarian American psychologist Mihaly Csikszentmihalyi. Flow is said to occur when you are consistently doing something you love and that you are good at, with the possible added benefit of bringing value to others' lives. Jeffrey Gaines, "The Philosophy Of Ikigai: Three Examples About Finding Purpose," 2020, https://positivepsychology.com/ikigai/

28 Abigail Brenner, "E~motions Of Change = Energy In Motion," 2011, https://www.psychologytoday.com/us/blog/in-flux/201106/emotions-change-energy-in-motion

29 "These Are The Top Ten Job Skills Of Tomorrow—And How Long It Takes To Learn Them," World Economic Forum, 2020, https://www.weforum.org/agenda/2020/10/top-10-work-skills-of-tomorrow-how-long-it-takes-to-learn-them/

30 This is based on data from emotional intelligence profiles for over a million workers from the frontlines to the C-suite. Travis Bradberry, "About Your Boss' Lack Of Emotional Intelligence," 2015, https://www.forbes.com/sites/travisbradberry/2015/02/03/about-your-boss-lack-of-emotional-intelligence/?sh=729cb0ed634d

31 Zawn Villines and William Berry, "What To Know About Toxic Positivity," Medical News Today, 2021, https://www.medicalnewstoday.com/articles/toxic-positivity

32 The theory that the human brain has evolved to protect us from dangers and focus on the negative is generally accepted. This negativity bias can be helpful at times and motivate us to keep moving forward, but negativity bias can also hold us back. The pressure to strive to be happy might be unrealistic at times, and acceptance might be a better approach. William Berry, "You Aren't Built To Be Happy: Evolutionary Psychology Suggests Brains Aren't Built For Consistent Happiness," 2019, https://www.psychologytoday.com/us/blog/the-second-noble-truth/201907/you-arent-built-be-happy

33 This article introduces the notion of culture-specific emotional intelligence (CSEI). Saurav Pathak, Etayankara Muralidharan, "Implications Of Culturally Implicit Perspective Of Emotional Intelligence," 2020, https://journals.sagepub.com/doi/abs/10.1177/1069397120938690

34 Nangyeon Lim, "Cultural differences in emotion: differences in emotional arousal level between the East and the West," 2016, https://www.ncbi.nlm.nih.gov/pmc/articles/PMC5381435/

35 This illustrates how we need to apply cultural context and not only apply a single lens on emotions. Anna Schouten, Michael Boiger, et al., "Cultural Differences In Emotion Suppression In Belgian And Japanese Couples: A Social Functional Model," *Frontiers In Psychology*, 2020, https://www.frontiersin.org/articles/10.3389/fpsyg.2020.01048/full#B37

36 This article highlights how leadership theories have not adequately captured social and emotional issues encountered by leaders within their social identity location. A qualitative study was used to examine the experiences of Black male leaders in an organizational setting using the frameworks of emotional intelligence and social architecture. Findings suggest that emotional intelligence explains why Black American leaders use specialized strategies to deal with

social and emotional distress, face barriers to acculturation into the workplace culture, and use code switching to navigate multiple identities. Enin Rudel, Brandi Derr, et al., "Emotional Intelligence, Organizational Social Architecture, And Black Male Leadership," *Advances In Developing Human Resources*, August 2021, https://www. researchgate.net/publication/354119488_Emotional_Intelligence_ Organizational_Social_Architecture_and_Black_Male_Leadership

37 P. Christopher Earley and Elaine Mosakowski, "Cultural Intelligence," *Harvard Business Review*, 2004, https://hbr.org/2004/10/ cultural-intelligence

38 Moh. Alifuddin and Widodo Widodo, "How Is Cultural Intelligence Related To Human Behavior?" *Journal Of Intelligence*, 2022, https:// www.ncbi.nlm.nih.gov/pmc/articles/PMC8788423/

39 Helen-Maria Lekas, Kerstin Pahl, and Crystal Fuller Lewis, "Rethinking Cultural Competence: Shifting to Cultural Humility," *Health Services Insights*, 2020, https://www.ncbi.nlm.nih.gov/pmc/articles/PMC7756036/

40 Carolina Herrando and Efthymios Constantinides, "Emotional Contagion: A Brief Overview And Future Directions," *Frontiers In Psychology*, 2021, https://www.ncbi.nlm.nih.gov/pmc/articles/PMC8322226/

41 A narcissist's presentation is deceiving and might include displays that seem like emotional intelligence. But authentic vulnerability involves disclosing uncomfortable and difficult emotions that are painful to admit. Erin Leonard, "Why A Narcissist May Seem Emotionally Intelligent: Three Factors Distinguish Machiavellian Tendencies From Sincere Vulnerability," *Psychology Today*, 2021, https://www.psychologytoday.com/us/blog/peaceful-parenting/202107/why-narcissist-may-seem-emotionally-intelligent

42 Where do you think you fit on the continuum? John Elder Robison, "The Limits Of Neurodiversity: Neurodiversity Is A Fresh Way To See Difference. Is It Right For You?," 2020, https://www.psychologytoday.com/us/blog/my-life-aspergers/202003/the-limits-neurodiversity

43 We are diverse in many ways, including in our brains. For example, what we call ADHD is, in most cases, just one end of a bell curve describing normal executive function. Neurodiversity, rather than being considered a disorder, should be viewed as a difference. Throughout your life, you may work with different people, and each person may process and learn information differently. It is important that we not only find common ground with each other, but that we also appreciate our differences. Ralph Lewis, "The Real Reason Everyone Seems To Have ADHD These Days: Seeing Adhd As One End Of A Normal Continuum Of Executive Function," *Psychology Today*, 2022, https://www.psychologytoday.com/us/blog/finding-purpose/202208/the-real-reason-everyone-seems-have-adhd-these-days

44 Young Hee Lee, Suk Hyung Bryan Lee, and Jong Yong Chung, "Research On How Emotional Expressions Of Emotional Labor Workers And Perception Of Customer Feedbacks Affect Turnover Intentions: Emphasis On Moderating Effects Of Emotional Intelligence," *Frontiers In Psychology*, 2019, https://www.frontiersin.org/articles/10.3389/fpsyg.2018.02526/full

45 The shadow as a concept comprises everything the conscious personality experiences as "negative." Jung emphasizes that we all have a shadow, and the shadow makes us human. "A Library Guide to Jung's Collected Works," Pacifica Graduate Library, https://pacifica.libguides.com/Jung/shadow

46 https://www.psychologytoday.com/us/basics/dark-triad

47 A sample of 87 organizational groups (297 employees and 87 supervisors) explains the association between SDT (supervisors' dark triad) and ratings of team outcomes. The frameworks claim that manipulative behaviors associated with high levels of SDT disturb the social fabric of the group and the balance of reciprocity in social exchanges at work." Oana C. Fodor, Petru L. Curșeu, and Nicoleta Meslec, "In Leaders We Trust, Or Should We? Supervisors' Dark Triad Personality Traits And Ratings Of Team Performance And Innovation," *Frontiers In Psychology*, 2021, https://www.ncbi.nlm.nih.gov/pmc/articles/PMC8236614/

48 While remote work may yield many benefits, one study showed the shift to firm-wide remote work caused business groups within Microsoft to initially become less interconnected. Longqi Yang, David Holtz, et al., "The Effects Of Remote Work On Collaboration Among Information Workers," *Nature Human Behaviour*, 2021, https://www.nature.com/articles/s41562-021-01196-4

49 Gratitude plays a key role in strengthening relationships. This study shows how expressions of gratitude improve teammates' cardiovascular stress responses compared to teams who did not express gratitude. Yumeng Gu, Joseph M. Ocampo, Sara B. Algoe, and Christopher Oveis, "Gratitude Expressions Improve Teammates' Cardiovascular Stress Responses," *Journal of Experimental Psychology: General*, 2022, https://pubmed.ncbi.nlm.nih.gov/35708951/

50 Mental illness can vary in impact, ranging from no impairment to mild, moderate, and even severe impairment, Mental Illness," National Institute of Mental Health, https://www.nimh.nih.gov/health/statistics/mental-illness

51 "Glenn Close Says She Wants To Change Stigma Of Mental Illness In Media: 'I Was Part Of It,'" Joanne Rose, *ABC News*, 2019, https://abc-news.go.com/Entertainment/glenn-close-character-fatal-attraction-contributed-stigma-mental/story?id=60938016

52 Workplace Health Promotion, Centers for Disease Control and Prevention, https://www.cdc.gov/workplacehealthpromotion/health-strategies/depression/evaluation-measures/index.html

53 Workplace Health Promotion, CDC.

54 Megan Leonhardt, "Us Workers Are Not Okay—And Employers Are Usually The Last To Know," *Fortune*, 2021, https://fortune.com/2021/09/20/us-workers-employers-anxiety-depression/

55 Anatomy Of Work Special Report: The Unexplored Link Between Imposter Syndrome And Burnout, https://resources.asana.com/americas-anatomy-of-work-burnout-ebook.html

56 Burnout is a syndrome conceptualized as resulting from chronic workplace stress that has not been successfully managed. It is characterized by three dimensions: (1) feelings of energy depletion or exhaustion; (2) increased mental distance from one's job, or feelings of negativism or cynicism related to one's job; and (3) reduced professional efficacy. "Burnout An 'Occupational Phenomenon': International Classification of Diseases," World Health Organization, 2019, https://www.who.int/news/item/28-05-2019-burn-out-an-occupational-phenomenon-international-classification-of-diseases

57 Amy Edmondson, "Psychological Safety And Learning Behavior In Work Teams," *Administrative Science Quarterly*, 1999, https://journals.sagepub.com/doi/abs/10.2307/2666999

58 How do you typically respond when someone asks, "How are you?" This question may seem like an informal greeting as opposed to a sincere request to open up and share. Leonhardt, "US Workers Are Not Okay."

59 Jessica Martino, Jennifer Pegg, and Elizabeth Pegg Frates, "The Connection Prescription: Using The Power Of Social Interactions And The Deep Desire For Connectedness To Empower Health And Wellness," *American Journal Of Lifestyle Medicine*, 2015, https://www.ncbi.nlm.nih.gov/pmc/articles/PMC6125010/.

60 Julianne Holt-Lunstad, Timothy Smith, and J. Bradley Layton, "Social Relationships and Mortality Risk: A Meta-analytic Review," 2010, PLoS Med 7(7): e1000316. https://doi.org/10.1371/journal.pmed.

61 Data shows that adults with mental health issues are more than twice as likely to experience loneliness as those with strong mental health. "The Loneliness Epidemic Persists: A Post-Pandemic Look At The State of Loneliness Among US Adults," 2022, Cigna, https://newsroom.cigna.com/loneliness-epidemic-persists-post-pandemic-look

62 Should we make decisions based on data, our gut, or a combination of the two? There are different philosophies and approaches to decision-making. While not infallible, our intuition can help us in complex decision-making. Kurt Matzler et al., "Intuitive Decision Making," *MIT Sloan Management Review*, 2007, https://www.researchgate.net/publication/233842234_Intuitive_Decision_Making

63 Dorothy Neufeld, "Waves Of Change: Understanding The Driving Force Of Innovation Cycles," World Economic Forum, 2021, https://www.weforum.org/agenda/2021/07/this-is-a-visualization-of-the-history-of-innovation-cycles/

64 Socially responsible automation is a framework to address the strong need to shape the future development of automation to help create a better world for people and society. Meera Sampath and Pramod P. Khargonekar, "Socially Responsible Automation: A Framework for Shaping the Future," *The Bridge*, 2018, https://www.nae.edu/200473/Socially-Responsible-Automation-A-Framework-for-Shaping-the-Future

65 This book provides an overview of AI and its potential impacts. As AI rapidly advances, we are at a pivotal time in history where the future of humanity rests upon key decisions. Henry A. Kissinger, Eric Schmidt, and Daniel Huttenlocher, *The Age Of AI: And Our Human Future* (New York: Little, Brown and Company, 2021).

66 Zawn Villines, "What A Flow State Is And How To Achieve It," MedicalNewsToday, 2022, https://www.medicalnewstoday.com/articles/flow-state

67 Although the definition of mind wandering is debated, it is generally considered to be pervasive in humans and likely has an important role to play across cognition, future planning, creative thinking, and problem-solving. Cornelia McCormick, Clive R. Rosenthal, et al., "Mind-Wandering In People With Hippocampal Damage," *Journal Of Neuroscience*, 2018, https://www.ncbi.nlm.nih.gov/pmc/articles/PMC5851780/#:~:text=It%20has%20been%20shown%20that,Smallwood%20and%20Schooler%2C%202015